PIVOT POINT

PIVOT POINT FUNDAMENTALS: COSMETOLOGY
HAIR DESIGN

1st Edition
4th Printing, October 2021
Printed in China

Pivot Point International, Inc.
Global Headquarters
8725 West Higgins Road, Suite 700
Chicago, IL 60631 USA

847-866-0500
pivot-point.com

61

CONTENTS
107ᶜ // HAIR DESIGN

168

92

48

229

142

33

2

107^c.1 |
HAIR DESIGN THEORY

EXPLORE //

What is usually wrong
when you say, "I'm
having a bad hair day"?

INSPIRE //

Understanding the wide range of temporary transformations possible in hair design will inspire your creativity.

ACHIEVE //

Following this lesson on *Hair Design Theory*, you'll be able to:

>> List three reasons clients receive hair design services

>> Identify two areas of hair design, and provide examples of each

>> Explain the three levels of observation used in hair design analysis

>> Summarize how sculpted forms are altered through hair design

>> Provide examples of shapes used in hair design setting patterns

>> Justify the value of creating different hair designs for the same client

FOCUS //

HAIR DESIGN THEORY

Hair Design Transformation

Hair Design Analysis

Hair Design's Influence on Sculpted Forms

Shapes in Hair Design

Change the Hair Design, Change the Effect

107ᶜ.1 | HAIR DESIGN THEORY

Hair design is arranging hair to create a temporary change in form, texture and direction of the finished design.

Altering texture and/or adding volume can change the entire feeling of a hair sculpture. Understanding how to analyze form, texture and direction of the hair— along with balance and proportion—are important design concepts for you to master. Hair designing is also known as hairstyling.

Just as a potter makes pottery, hair designers use the medium of hair to express their artistic vision. Only the boundaries of your imagination can limit your creative expression.

HAIR DESIGN TRANSFORMATION

The transformations you create in hair design can range from subtle to dramatic. Whether offered as a stand-alone service, or in conjunction with another salon service, hair design is important because it is the finish that influences how your clients look when they leave the salon. Keep in mind that while the sculpture lays the foundation for works of art, hair design provides design versatility. Following are reasons why clients receive hair design services.

1. **THE FINISH**

   To complete another service, such as a sculpture or color. Clients generally expect to replicate the finish at home.

2. **WEEKLY OR BIWEEKLY SERVICE**

   To create a hair design that lasts until the next appointment. Clients expect little or no maintenance until the next appointment.

3. **SPECIAL OCCASION**

   To create a hair design for the client who is attending a special or formal occasion, such as a wedding. Clients cannot generally replicate the design at home.

HAIR DESIGN SERVICES

There are two areas of hair design services, wet and thermal. Each includes specific techniques and skill sets, and each is adapted to meet the individual needs of the client.

» **Wet design refers to the area of hair designing in which the hair is manipulated into the desired shapes and movements while wet and then allowed to dry; also known as wet styling.**

» **Thermal designing is the technique of drying and/or designing hair by using a hand-held dryer while simultaneously using your fingers, a variety of brushes, pressing comb and/or thermal irons; also known as thermal styling.**

Wet Design	Thermal Design
» Structured, longer lasting finish	» Softer casual finish
» Requires drying time under a hood dryer	» Generally includes air forming

MOLDING

AIR FORMING

FINGERWAVING

FLAT IRONING

ROLLER/PINCURL SET

PRESSING/CURLING

Wet and thermal design skills are often used during the preparation of a long hair design service. For more information refer to lessons in *Long Hair.*

HAIR DESIGN ANALYSIS

It is important to sharpen your observational skills to analyze the design you envisioned before creating it. There are three levels of observation, or primary design considerations, that are used to analyze a hair design.

>> Basic – Form/Shape
>> Detail – Texture
>> Abstract – Direction

When creating hair designs, you will need to consider the whole design as well as its separate parts. Analyzing a hair design using basic, detail and abstract levels of observation provides you with a foundation to re-create what you see. As your observation and analysis skills increase, your ability to envision your own unique designs will grow.

BASIC – FORM/SHAPE

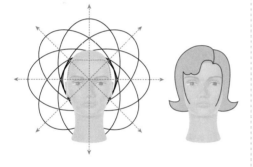

>> View the three-dimensional form from all directions

>> Determine where volume (mass or fullness) is positioned

>> Determine where indentation (hollowness) is positioned

>> Identify the outer shape, such as circular or triangular

DETAIL – TEXTURE

>> Look at the overall surface texture
   ▪ Unactivated (smooth)
   ▪ Activated (rough)
   ▪ Combination

>> Identify the types of textures you see
   ▪ Straight
   ▪ Wavy
   ▪ Curly
   ▪ Tightly curled
   ▪ Crimped
   ▪ Combination

ABSTRACT – DIRECTION

>> Observe the overall direction in which the hair is moving

>> Identify the directions within the form

SALON**CONNECTION**

Walking Advertisement

Hair designing can "make or break" the success of the other services you perform in the salon. You may create a technically perfect haircut or a great color, but if you are not able to "finish" the design successfully, your client may not appreciate your initial skills. Offering a variety of styling options, teaching your client how to reproduce the style at home and how to use finishing products, builds client loyalty and satisfaction!

BASIC – FORM AND SHAPE

In hair design, form is the result of:

>> Volume
>> Indentation

The form of a design can expand in any direction. Analyzing the position of volume and indentation from all angles allows you to view the outer shape of the design.

When analyzing form, people naturally try to find equilibrium within the design. Developing a sense of balance in any art form requires strong observational skills as well as intuition. Balance, whether symmetrical or asymmetrical, plays an integral part in the dynamics of a design and must be analyzed from all angles.

PERIMETER EXPANSION

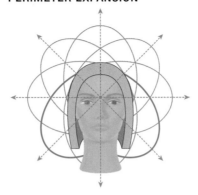

EXPANSION AT THE SIDES

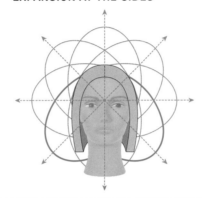

EXPANSION AT THE TOP

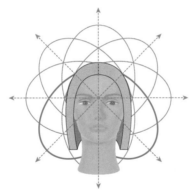

DISCOVER**MORE**

Blow Dry Bars

If hair design is the only area of cosmetology you wish to focus on, then you are in luck! Today, blow dry bars are ever so popular. These types of bars cater to clients who just want to have their hair shampooed and blow dried, or straightened. Many of these blow dry bars know how to spoil clients as they sit back and enjoy a film while having their hair styled. Search the Internet for blow dry bars to see what services they offer, and perhaps pamper yourself. As a client, you can "research," learn how professionals communicate, and in turn, gain communication ideas yourself!

DETAIL – TEXTURE

Texture has a strong influence on the total design. Some texture changes expand the form or change the direction of the hair. Identifying the texture will determine the finishing technique or type of tool required to create the desired finish. Your client's natural texture, whether it is straight, wavy, curly or tightly curled, can be temporarily changed through wet design or thermal design.

Texture Character

The texture character refers to the shape of the texture pattern and is created by the shape of the tool and the position of the tool along the hairstrand. Texture patterns include:

>> Straight
>> Waves
>> Curls
>> Spiral curls
>> Crimped

UNACTIVATED SURFACE TEXTURE

PATTERN	TOOLS
STRAIGHT	FLAT IRONING
STRAIGHT	PRESSING COMB

ACTIVATED SURFACE TEXTURE

PATTERN	TOOLS
WAVES	AIR FORMING WITH BRUSH
CURLS	ROLLERS
SPIRAL CURLS	CURLING IRON
CRIMPED TEXTURES	CRIMPING IRON

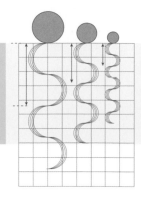

Length Reduction – Note the shrinkage factor that results from various size tools used on the same length of hair.

Texture Speed

Texture speed or activation describes the dimension of the texture pattern, and can range from slow waves to fast, highly activated curls. The texture speed is achieved by the number of times the hair wraps around a tool, and in relation to the length of hair. Large diameter tools used on longer lengths produce large waves and are considered slow, while smaller diameter tools produce tighter curls and are considered fast.

A LONG, SLOW WAVE **A MEDIUM-SPEED CURL** **A FAST-SPEED CURL PATTERN**

ABSTRACT – DIRECTION

The overall direction of a design can be analyzed according to where the hair moves in relation to the face. Directions are often described as:

>> Hair moving forward, or toward the face

>> Back, or away from the face

>> To one side

>> Any combination of these

The direction in which the hair is worn can make a major change in a client's appearance.

TOWARD THE FACE **AWAY FROM THE FACE**

Direction Within the Design

Besides the overall design direction, directional changes within the design can also be analyzed. These directional changes are lines that can be straight, curved or angled. They lead the eye through the design, giving the impression of motion.

HAIR DESIGN'S INFLUENCE ON SCULPTED FORMS

Hair design techniques allow you to temporarily alter the shape, texture and direction of your client's sculpted form.

For example:
» Shift the position of weight within the sculpture to create a new shape
» Alter the existing texture by adding waves, curls or crimped texture in a given area or throughout
» Change the direction, with a center or side part, or move the hair toward or away from the face

SOLID FORM

The hallmark of the solid form is the unactivated surface texture and perimeter weight line. Design decisions can range from smooth silky finishes, to face-framing soft waves, to curly textures throughout. Keep in mind, that the tighter the curl pattern, the more expansive the form becomes. The addition of curls throughout, shifts the weight area upward creating the illusion of a layered form.

GRADUATED FORM

Graduated forms consist of a combination of unactivated and activated textures, with a weight area occurring where the two textures meet. The inherent width and expansion of the graduated form can further be accentuated by adding wavy or curly texture patterns. Tighter curl patterns produce wider silhouettes and emphasize the triangular shape of the graduated form.

INCREASE-LAYERED FORM

Increase-layered forms consist of lengths that disperse throughout the form with no discernible weight resulting in an oval shape. Design decisions can range from directional movement such as face-framing layers toward the face, to layers that move away from the face. The overall shape and length of the increase-layered form can be drastically altered with the introduction of tighter curl patterns. Notice how tighter curl patterns cause a length reduction and the illusion of shorter lengths.

UNIFORMLY LAYERED FORM

The totally activated, round shape of the uniformly layered form has no discernible weight. Uniformly layered forms can be finished from a side part, styled away from or toward the face. Styling options range from smooth soft flicks of texture to break up the rounded shape, to elongating the shape by adding volume in one area while reducing it in another, to adding curls throughout to emphasize the rounded shape.

COMBINATION FORMS

Options for combination form designs range from smooth unactivated finishes that showcase the sculpted forms, to soft wavy shapes or curly finishes that defy gravity. Use your imagination for the right client and dramatically change the overall form.

SHAPES IN HAIR DESIGN

Geometric shapes are the foundation of design and are incorporated in setting patterns. Understanding the characteristics of each shape helps you to create the desired direction and movement of the hair. Both straight and curved shapes are used and often combined within one design. Refer to the lesson on *Hair Design Skills* for more information on shapes.

STRAIGHT SHAPES

Straight shapes create straight directional movement either away from the face, or toward the face.

Straight shapes include:

>> Rectangles
>> Triangles

Rectangles

The hair within a rectangle shape will usually move in one direction.

Triangles

The hair within triangle shapes can disperse outward from the narrow end of the triangle. Or the hair can disperse from the wide end toward the point.

CURVATURE SHAPES

Curvature shapes create curved movement in the hair either in a clockwise or counterclockwise direction. Curvature shapes include:

>> Circles
>> Oblongs

Circles

The circle shape is most often subdivided into half- or quarter-circles. The half-circle shown here is set with rollers to move half the hair away from the face, and half toward the face, creating a side fringe.

Oblongs

Two or more oblongs that alternate directions create wave patterns. Oblongs can be molded or set with rollers or pincurls.

CHANGE THE HAIR DESIGN, CHANGE THE EFFECT

The temporary nature of form, texture and direction changes produced during a hair design not only provides you with creative opportunities, it also provides clients with:

>> Freedom to change their look as often as they like without a chemical commitment

>> More options for styling their favorite haircut

>> The flexibility to try new designs just for fun or for special occasions

Below are examples of two very different hairstyles achieved based on the same model with the same sculpture, using different finishing techniques. Keep in mind, that although clients may not always be able to exactly duplicate the designs at home, you can teach them tips and tricks to achieve a similar style.

1. Smooth air forming with the appropriate finishing products creates a sleek shiny finish.

2. Air-formed waves at the fringe and scrunched curl texture highlights and enhances this client's natural curl pattern.

1. Smooth air-formed flicks of texture creates an airy finish.

2. Adding large curls with the curling iron expands the form and creates a romantic feeling.

1. Structured longer lasting finishes are achieved through roller sets. Defined directional movement creates a classic finish.

2. Breaking up the texture with your fingers, along with the use of product, allows you to alter the finish to create casual curls.

Whether you are finishing a hair sculpture, providing a weekly service or creating a design for that special occasion, transforming your client's hair using wet or thermal design techniques can help you build a loyal clientele. Remember, the shape of your client's hair sculpture serves as the foundation for your design creativity!

LESSONS LEARNED

The reasons you will be performing hair design services are:

» As a finish to complete another salon service

» As a weekly or biweekly service

» For a special occasion design

The two areas of hair design are:

» Wet design – Molding, fingerwaving and setting the hair with rollers and/or pincurls

» Thermal design – Air forming, thermal ironing and/or flat ironing and pressing and curling

The three levels of observation used during hair design analysis are:

» Basic – Form and shape – Consider from all directions where volume and indentation are positioned

» Detail – Texture – Overall surface appearance to include:
  ▪ Activated
  ▪ Unactivated

» Abstract – Direction – Includes the overall direction the hair is moving in and the directions within the form

Sculpted forms can be altered to include:

» Solid Form – Accentuating the perimeter weight area or by adding texture throughout

» Graduated Form – Enhancing the two types of texture by adding curl textures that further expand the silhouette or triangular shape

» Increase-layered form – Creating directional movement toward or away from the face, or by adding texture within a given area which can dramatically alter the oval shape

» Uniformly layered form – Creating soft-flicks of texture to break-up the rounded shape, or adding texture throughout to further enhance the rounded shape

Shapes used in hair design help you control the direction and movement of the hair.

» Straight shapes include:
  ▪ Rectangle
  ▪ Triangle

» Curved shapes include:
  ▪ Circle
  ▪ Oblong

Hair designing as a service offers the client:

» Freedom to change their look as often as they like without a commitment to chemicals

» More options for styling their favorite sculpture

» The flexibility to try new looks just for fun, or for special occasions

HAIR DESIGN TOOLS
AND ESSENTIALS | 107^c.2

EXPLORE //

How do you think the size or shape of a tool can affect the final outcome of a hairstyle?

INSPIRE //

Strong straight lines, soft
undulating waves, bouncing
curls and crimped textures—
all are possible with the right
tool and product choice!

ACHIEVE //

Following this lesson on *Hair Design Tools
and Essentials*, you'll be able to:

>> Describe the function of a variety of combs and brushes
used in hair design

>> Describe the function of a variety of wet design tools

>> Describe the function of a variety of thermal design tools

>> Provide examples of supplies, products and equipment
used to perform a hair design

FOCUS //

**HAIR DESIGN TOOLS
AND ESSENTIALS**

Combs and Brushes

Wet Design Tools

Thermal Design Tools

Hair Design Essentials

107ᶜ.2 | HAIR DESIGN TOOLS AND ESSENTIALS

Tools play an important role in the creation of a hair design. They help you achieve the temporary changes in form, direction and texture you desire. These tools include combs, brushes and wet and thermal design tools. Each tool is unique and creates a specific texture pattern in the hair. Understanding the various types of tools and their function is key for the success of any hair design. Electrical and stove-heated tools should be handled with care to ensure yours and your clients' safety. Hair design essentials include the supplies, products and equipment used throughout hair design services.

Remember that the combination of the three design elements—form, texture and color—creates a final design. As you create temporary changes in texture and form, using various tools and products, consider how the existing color pattern influences the final design and can be more or less visible depending on how the hair is finished. Smooth texture patterns increase the visibility of color placement.

COMBS AND BRUSHES

COMBS

The main features of a comb are its size and the spacing between its teeth. Some combs have a pointed end, called the tail, which is used to part or lift the hair. When a comb has widely spaced teeth, the resulting texture patterns in the hair reflect the shape and interval of the teeth.

TOOLS		FUNCTION
Molding Comb		>> Used to distribute and mold the hair >> Used in fingerwaving >> Includes both wide-spaced teeth to distribute the hair and fine-spaced teeth to refine the lines of distribution
Master Sketcher Comb		>> Used for backcombing and smoothing the surface of the hair >> Used to detangle the hair
Fine-Tooth Tail Comb		>> Used for distribution, molding, scaling and parting the hair >> The fine-spaced teeth firmly grasp the hair to distribute the hair smoothly >> Also known as drawing comb
Wide-Tooth Tail Comb		>> Used for backcombing and finishing techniques >> The wide-spaced teeth create texture patterns that reflect the shape and interval of the teeth >> Detangles >> Separates curls and defines texture >> Also known as rake comb
Lifter Comb		>> Used for backcombing >> Details surface texture >> Lifts and adds volume >> Also known as teaser and lift comb

BRUSHES

The main features of a brush are its size, shape and bristles. Some brushes have a round barrel, while some have a flat, padded or hard base. Brushes can consist of nylon or boar bristles.

TOOLS		FUNCTION
 7- or 9-Row Brush		>> Used to air form smoother textures or create directional emphasis >> 7- or 9-row brush – Smooths wavy or curly textures; creates volume and curved end texture
 Vent Brush		>> Vent brush – Allows the greatest airflow to the hair so that the lengths can be dried quickly while directing them into the lines of the design
 Round Brushes		>> Used to create volume, curved end texture or curls >> Available in different diameters, with different types and spacing of bristles >> Bristle types include nylon and boar >> May have a metal core that retains heat to strengthen the curl pattern >> Some may have a wood or plastic core
 Cushion Brush		>> Used to brush hair, or on dry hair to relax a set, dry mold, backbrush or smooth the surface of the hair >> Consists of a soft, padded base >> Bristles may be nylon or boar >> The type, density and length of the bristles on a brush will influence the surface appearance

WET DESIGN TOOLS

Wet design tools are used to manipulate the hair into the desired shapes and movements while wet, after which the hair is allowed to dry. Wet design tools include various types, sizes and shapes of rollers.

ROLLERS

Rollers are applied to wet or damp hair. The hair must be dried with these tools still in place to achieve the desired texture pattern. Wet sets using rollers have a more structured finish than self-adhering rollers or hot rollers. Rollers include gripper-type surfaces or metallic.

TOOLS		FUNCTION
 Cylinder (Straight) Rollers		>> Available in a range of lengths and diameters >> Create uniform curl formation across length/width of roller >> Cylinder rollers are used within straight shapes, such as rectangles and triangles >> A faster way to set hair than using volume or stand-up pincurls to achieve the same effect
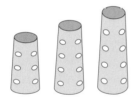 Conical or Cone-Shaped Rollers		>> Available in a range of lengths and diameters >> Consist of a progression of speeds because of their wide and narrow ends; creates progression of curl diameter >> Cone-shaped rollers are used in curvature shapes, such as circles and oblongs

Refer to the lessons on *Infection Control* and *Hair Design Guest Experience* for information on proper cleaning and disinfecting procedures used for tools, supplies and equipment.

THERMAL DESIGN TOOLS

Thermal design tools are heated tools that are used to dry or design hair into the desired shape and texture. "Thermal" means relating to or caused by heat. It is important to remember that heat is a form of energy that needs to be handled with great care, especially when used on hair.

TOOLS		FUNCTION

Blow Dryer and Attachments		>> Blow dryer – Used to air form wet hair while using brushes, combs and your fingers to create temporary direction and texture changes
		  ▪ May include multiple heat/speed combinations and a cooling button
		
		>> Attachments:
		  ▪ Concentrators – Focus the airflow to a small area; come in a variety of sizes
		
		  ▪ Diffusers spread a gentle airflow over larger areas and are used for creating scrunched textures

Curling Irons		>> Use heat to create temporary curvilinear texture patterns >> Some have individual electric cords, some are cordless >> Some acquire heat from an electric base or stove >> Professional curling irons, also referred to as marcel irons, come in a variety of diameters
Pressing Comb		>> Used to apply heat and tension to temporarily straighten tightly curled hair >> Heated with an electric base or stove
Flat Iron		>> Consists of two flat plates >> Hair is positioned between the heated plates to temporarily straighten and silk the hair >> Some include an electric cord >> Some may be heated with an electric stove >> Plates include ceramic and metal

TOOLS	FUNCTION
 Crimping Iron	» Consists of angular or serrated plates » When heated, are used to create crimped texture or a zigzag pattern » May include an electric cord » Some may be heated with an electric base
 Undulating Iron	» Consists of two undulating or curved irons » Used to create an "S" pattern or wave formation » Some include an electric cord » Some may be heated with an electric base or stove
 Hot Comb/Brush	» Used to dry, smooth or curl hair simultaneously » Some include air forced over a heating element » Teeth or brush direct hair into new pattern, sometimes referred to as air waving
Hot Rollers	» Hot rollers are used on dry hair to quickly add volume and texture » Tools are heated electrically, or with steam, and applied to hair » Secured with roller clips » Tool and hair must be cooled before tools are removed » Follow disinfection guidelines provided by your area's regulatory agency
 Self-Adhering Rollers	» Self-adhering rollers can be applied to dry hair to reinforce the curl during or after a blow dry service, or a hooded dryer may be used » Adds soft textural movement » Applying setting spray to hair prior to setting will strengthen the curl result » Follow disinfection guidelines provided by your area's regulatory agency

SALON**CONNECTION**

Stay Current

New tools and products enter the market quite frequently. It's up to you to stay current with the various types and function each tool and product has to offer. Remember, your clients depend on you to educate them on the type of tool and product they should use to achieve the desired look. Special consideration should be given to their hair type, texture and density to ensure a successful recommendation!

HAIR DESIGN ESSENTIALS

The following charts will help you become familiar with the various supplies, products and equipment you will use in the salon.

>> Hair design supplies include single-use items, such as neck strips and multi-use items, such as capes, clips and towels.

>> Hair design, or styling, products are used to add a range of support and texture to the hair. When choosing styling products, consider the end result and visual effect that you and your client wish to achieve. Then, choose a product based on the function it serves. Keep in mind that although products may be designed for a specific effect, and to be applied to dry, damp and/or wet hair, it is up to you as a designer to learn how to effectively use products to achieve the desired look for your client. In some instances, you may need to layer several products to get a desired result, while in other cases one product will do the trick!

>> The characteristics of styling products include:
   - Viscosity – Liquids to solids
   - Level of shine – Matte to high shine
   - Level of hold/control – Light to super firm

Keep in mind that the fragrance of a product plays a key role in whether or not you select a particular product for your client! Be sure to allow your client to become familiar with the aroma of a product before you apply it to their hair.

>> Hair design equipment includes the furnishings/fixtures, such as the styling chair, hood dryer and shampoo bowl necessary for a professional hair design service.

HAIR DESIGN SUPPLIES

SUPPLIES	FUNCTION
Picks	Secure rollers (ribbed surface) in place while hair dries
Double-Prong Clips	Secure rollers (smooth surface) in place while hair dries
Single-Prong Clips	Secure pincurls in place while hair dries
Wave/Styling Clamp	Holds fingerwaves in place while hair dries
Neck Strip	Protects client's skin from contact with the cape
Plastic Cape	Protects client's clothing during the shampoo service
Cloth Cape	Protects client's clothing during a combout service; replaces the plastic cape
Spatula	Used to remove product from containers; single-use
Water Bottle	Holds water; used to keep the hair damp as needed during hair design services

HAIR DESIGN PRODUCTS

PRODUCTS	FUNCTION
Gel	» Creates maximum control, support and structure » Used for wet-looking finishes, wet-setting, molding and styling » Firmer hold than lotion
Spray Gel	» Supports volume and movement » Used for wet-looking finishes » Enhances and defines curls
Mousse	» Supports volume and movement » Used to define texture and directional patterns » Foam consistency » May contain conditioners
Creams/Lotions	» Smooth and soften hair » Control frizz » Define curls » May contain moisturizers
Oils/Serums	» Control frizz » Smooth cuticle
Pomade	» Creates sleek, smooth finishes
Wax	» Creates natural, spiky and rough textures
Paste	» Adds styling control, texture definition and separation
Fiber	» Adds styling control, texture definition and separation
Putty	» Creates chunky texture separation
Clay	» Adds texture definition and support
Powders/Dusts	» Add volume, hold and/or texture
Non-Aerosol Hairspray	» Holds finished design in place » Liquid dispensed through a pump
Aerosol Hairspray	» Holds finished design in place » Liquid dispensed through compressed gas and spray
Pressing Oil/Cream	» Prepares and protects hair during pressing service and excessive blow drying » Helps prevent scorching and breakage » Conditions and adds shine » Helps hair stay pressed longer » Use less pressing oil to avoid smoke or burning while pressing hair
Thermal Protectant	» Prepares and protects hair against heat styling » Conditions and adds shine

HAIR DESIGN EQUIPMENT

EQUIPMENT	FUNCTION
Hair Design Station	Provides a place for tools to be displayed and organized
Hydraulic Chair	Provides proper back support for a client during the service; adjustable
Hood Dryer	Used during a wet styling service to dry the hair (molding, rollers and/or pincurls)
Shampoo Bowl	Supports client's neck and holds water and shampoo products during a shampoo service
Disinfectant Container	Holds solution for disinfecting tools

Refer to the *Shampoo and Scalp Massage Theory* lesson for information on proper draping procedures.

Refer to the *Hair Care Product Knowledge* lesson for information on shampoos and conditioners.

DISCOVERMORE

Master Your Tools!

Did you know that pottery is made by forming a clay material such as earthenware, stoneware or porcelain into various shapes, then heating them at high temperatures in what is known as a kiln to set the shapes into a permanent state? A potter not only molds the clay material, but decorates it using various tools. Artists know how to use specific materials and tools to achieve various effects. As a hair designer, it's up to you to become a master of the tools and products that are available to create customized finishes for your unique clients. Search the Internet for creative hairstyles, and share how you think those styles were achieved with your classmates!

Adapting unique designs for your client, such as smooth silky finishes, flowing air-formed lengths, structured roller sets and spiky trendy designs are all possible when you apply your skills of hair design tools and products.

LESSONS LEARNED

The main combs and brushes used in hair design and their function include:

>> Molding comb – Used to distribute and mold hair

>> Master Sketcher – Used to backcomb and smooth the surface of the hair

>> Fine-tooth tail comb – Used for distribution, molding, parting and scaling

>> Wide-tooth tail comb – Used for backcombing and finishing techniques

>> Vent and 7- and 9-row brushes – Used during air forming to create directional movement and add volume

>> Round brushes – Used during air forming to create volume, curved end texture and curls

>> Cushion brushes – Used to relax a set, backbrush or smooth the surface of the hair

Wet design tools and their function that are used in a hair design include:

>> Cylinder rollers – Used within straight shapes, such as rectangles and triangles

>> Conical or cone-shaped rollers – Used in curvature shapes, such as half-circle and oblongs

Thermal tools used in hair design and their function include:

>> Blow dryer – Used to dry wet hair with the use of your fingers, combs or brushes

>> Curling iron – Creates temporary curvilinear texture patterns

>> Pressing comb – Temporarily straightens tightly curled hair

>> Flat iron – Straightens hair

>> Undulating iron – Creates an undulating wave pattern

>> Crimping iron – Creates crimped texture

In addition to the hair design tools, hair design essentials include the supplies, products and equipment that are needed to perform a hair design service:

>> Supplies include single-use items, such as neck strips and spatulas, and multi-use items, such as picks, clips, capes and towels

>> Products are used to add support and texture to hair. The characteristics of styling products include:
  ▪ Viscosity – Liquids to solids
  ▪ Level of shine – Matte to high shine
  ▪ Level of hold/control – Light to super firm

>> Hair design equipment includes the permanent furnishings and fixtures, such as the styling chair, hood dryer and shampoo bowl

HAIR DESIGN SKILLS

107ᶜ.3

EXPLORE //

What can happen if you build something for the first time, but don't follow the step-by-step procedures?

INSPIRE //

Whether you're a fashion designer, interior designer or hair designer, envisioning and following a plan will help create predictable results.

FOCUS //

HAIR DESIGN SKILLS

Setting Procedures

Finishing Procedures

ACHIEVE //

Following this lesson on *Hair Design Skills*, you'll be able to:

>> Describe the setting procedures used in hair design

>> Describe the finishing procedures used in hair design

107ᶜ.3 | HAIR DESIGN SKILLS

Imagine that you are asked to add "surface texture" to a house that has just been built. How and where would you begin? You might begin with an understanding that the house will serve as the foundation. You will be building upon a form that has been established. Then, you might define the style of the house to ensure the new surface pattern reflects the personality of the house. Then, you might decide on materials to use: brick, siding or wood.

Similarly, a hair sculpture will serve as the foundation for a hair design. Next, you might think about and envision the various types of textures and movements you wish to create. Finally, you will consider the tools you can choose from and how you would use them to create the desired results.

As an artist, it is recommended that you learn to first visualize a design before creating it. Once you know **what** you want to achieve, following step-by-step procedures will help you determine **how** to achieve it. In this lesson, we will take a look at setting and finishing procedures that are used to create designs and ensure consistent, predictable results.

Hair design procedures fall into two main categories:

>> Setting procedures

>> Finishing procedures

SETTING PROCEDURES

Whether you are setting hair with rollers or pincurls, air forming or using a curling iron, the procedures you'll use are very similar. The techniques and tools will vary, but the principles behind setting the hair remain the same. Depending on the technique you choose, some of these procedures will be performed simultaneously, while others will be omitted as determined by your design decisions.

The setting procedures that lead to predictable results are:
1. Distribute
2. Mold
3. Scale
4. Part
5. Apply

WET-SETTING PROCEDURES

| Distribute | Mold | Scale | Part | Apply |

THERMAL SETTING PROCEDURES

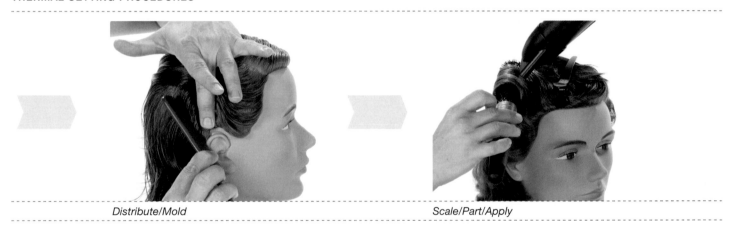

| Distribute/Mold | Scale/Part/Apply |

In some instances, such as with air forming, multiple procedures are performed simultaneously.

DISCOVER**MORE**

Keep it Simple! One Piece at a Time, One Step at a Time.
Have you ever tried to put a 1,000-piece puzzle together all in one step? Probably not. Puzzles are generally put together one piece, one step at a time. Whether you work from the outside edges inward, or from the inside out, both plans result in a complete puzzle. When creating a hair design, understanding how to connect the pieces or shapes helps you complete the composition one step at a time. Search the Internet to discover how other artists break compositions into smaller, easier steps. Share your findings and think about the different approaches the next time you "design" a composition for your client.

DISTRIBUTE

Distribution is the direction the hair is combed or dispersed over the curve of the head. Distribution begins from one or several points of origin. A point of origin is the place where the motion begins, or the beginning of the movement within a shape or design.

MOLD

Once the hair is distributed in the desired direction, it is molded. To **mold** or **shape** the hair refers to designing wet hair in straight or curved lines to create a pattern. By molding the hair, designers map out the direction the hair will move to reflect the lines featured in the finished design.

Types of Distribution

PARALLEL DISTRIBUTION

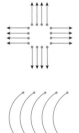

>> Straight or curved lines that are distributed from *multiple* points of origin and travel at an equal distance from one another

>> Curved parallel lines result from distributing the hair in a curved motion while molding

RADIAL DISTRIBUTION

>> Straight or curved lines that originate from a *single* point of origin and radiate outward in any direction, like the spokes of a wheel

>> Radial lines are distributed and then curved while molding

Molding as a Finished Design

MOLD AND DRY

Some finished designs are the result of distributing and molding wet hair after a styling product has been applied. The hair can be dried and combed out or left molded to create a "wet look."

HAIR WRAPPING

A setting pattern, known as hair wrapping, involves molding the hair around the head. The smooth, curvature finish reflects the curves of the head.

SCALE

To **scale** or section means to carve out shapes in the proper size and proportion to establish the direction and the lines of the design.

Scaling considerations:

>> Scaling is done to ensure that the tools fit properly, and it serves as a blueprint for the design.

>> Shapes are scaled according to the desired proportion and desired movement in the hair.

>> The tip of a tail comb is used to scale a shape.

>> The size of the client's head and individual growth patterns will influence the size of the shapes that are scaled.

At first, a tool is used to determine the correct size to scale the shape. Eventually, you will be able to trust your eye to scale the correct size.

In hair design, geometric shapes are the components that make up a composition. Understanding the characteristics of each shape helps you create the desired directions and movements within a design.

Straight Shapes

Straight shapes create straight directional movement away from the face or toward the face. They are generally combined with curvature shapes to create an infinite number of hair design compositions.

Straight shapes or sections include:
>> Rectangles
>> Triangles
>> Trapezoids
>> Diamonds and Kites

RECTANGLE

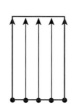

>> Begins with parallel straight distribution

>> Once shape is distributed and molded, it's scaled with a tail comb according to desired size

TRIANGLE

>> Begins with radial distribution

>> A tail comb is used to distribute hair from a single point of origin

>> Parallel distribution is used to distribute hair within the triangle

>> Once shape is molded it's scaled with a tail comb according to desired size

TRAPEZOID

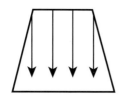

>> A straight shape that includes two parallel and two nonparallel sides

>> Consists of parallel distribution

>> Often not scaled, since it's formed by remaining hair to blend into other shapes

DIAMOND AND KITE

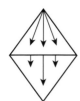
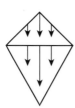

>> Shapes can be combined to encompass a larger area

>> Back-to-back triangles create diamond or kite shapes, which relate well to top or back of head

>> Narrow-to-wide triangles begin with radial distribution

>> Wide-to-narrow triangles begin with parallel distribution

Curvature Shapes

Curvature (curved) shapes imply motion and are generally used to create curvature directions or waves. Curvature shapes can be distributed in either a clockwise or counterclockwise direction. These shapes include circles, ovals and oblongs.

CLOCKWISE

COUNTERCLOCKWISE

  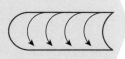

CIRCLE

A **circle** is a geometric, closed-curve shape bound by a circumference and having equal radii from a center point of origin. Generally, only a portion of the circle—such as a half-circle—is used.

Half-Circle

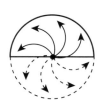  

>> Used to move hair in equal proportions from a center point of origin

>> Straight radial lines are used from a single point of origin to establish position of half-circle

>> Curved radial lines are molded to create half-circle shape in clockwise or counterclockwise direction

>> Shape is scaled according to desired size

>> A tool may be used as a guide to scale shape

Expanded Circle

 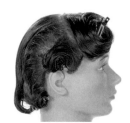

>> Used to encompass a larger area than half-circle

>> Same distribution and molding rules apply as half-circle, except a larger area is scaled according to area you wish to encompass

>> Circle is further subdivided into inner and outer circle for control, resulting in both radial and parallel distribution

OVAL

An **oval** is a geometric curved shape bound by a circumference, having unequal radii from a point of origin. Generally, only a portion of the oval–such as the half-oval–is used.

Half-Oval

>> Used to move hair in unequal proportions from an off-center point of origin

>> Unequal radial lines produce fast-to-slow speeds that result in unequal movements from point of origin

>> Shorter radial lines produce faster speeds, while the longer radial lines produce slower speeds

>> Hair is distributed in straight lines from an off-center point of origin

>> Shape is then molded in a clockwise or counterclockwise direction and scaled according to desired size

Expanded Oval

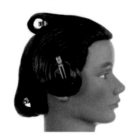

>> Extension of half-oval

>> Used to encompass a larger area than half-oval

>> Same distribution and molding rules apply as half-oval, except a larger area is scaled according to area you wish to encompass

OBLONGS

For the purposes of hair design, an **oblong** is an elongated curvature shape with parallel "C" lines, consisting of a convex (closed) end and a concave (open) end.

Oblongs

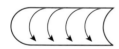

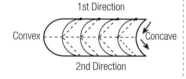

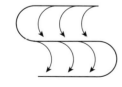

>> Contain multiple points of origin and parallel curved distribution

>> Consist of a 1st and 2nd direction

>> 1st direction, or top half of shape, moves toward convex end

>> 2nd direction, or bottom half of shape, moves toward concave end

>> Scaled according to desired size or tool to be used for setting

>> When two oblong shapings alternate, an "S-shaped" wave pattern is created

PART

After molding and scaling the design, the hair is parted and subdivided for control. **Partings are lines that subdivide shapes or sections to help distribute and control the hair.** Partings can be parallel, radial, horizontal, diagonal or vertical and are used to create the subsections often referred to as bases. The base is the area where you apply various tools and techniques.

Parallel Horizontal Partings

RECTANGLE-SHAPED BASES

Parallel horizontal partings are used within a rectangle shape to create rectangle-shaped bases.

TRIANGLE- AND TRAPEZOID-SHAPED BASES

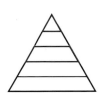 

Parallel horizontal partings can also be used within a triangle shape to create trapezoid-shaped bases.

Radial Partings

TRIANGLE-SHAPED BASES

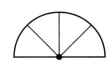 

TRAPEZOID-SHAPED BASES

A radial parting pattern is used within curvature shapes like the circle to create triangle-shaped bases in the inner circle and trapezoid-shaped bases in the outer circle; triangle-shaped bases are created in an oval.

Parallel Diagonal Partings

RHOMBOID-SHAPED BASES

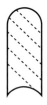 

>> A rhomboid is a straight shape with two sets of parallel lines and no right angles.

>> Parallel diagonal partings (45° angles) are used to create rhomboid-shaped bases within an oblong.

APPLY

Once straight- or curved-shaped sections are parted, the hair is set by applying a tool such as a roller, round brush or curling iron. This will produce the desired amount of volume, indentation and degree of texture and movement.

Tool Choice

Defined curls and waves are achieved by applying:
>> Rollers
>> Thermal irons
>> Round brushes
>> Pincurls

Size of Curl

The size of the curl will be determined by the:
>> Diameter of the tool
>> Diameter of a pincurl

Tools with smaller diameters create tighter or faster curls, while larger-diameter tools produce slow waves.

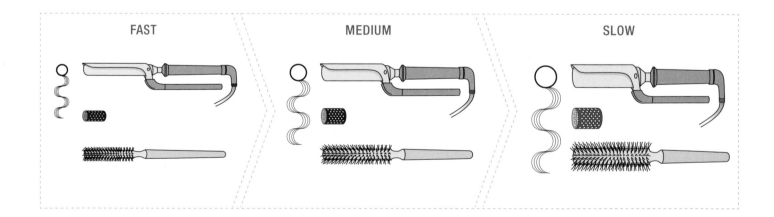

FAST · MEDIUM · SLOW

Refer to *Straight Volume and Indentation* and *Curvature Volume and Indentation* lessons to learn more on base controls.

Components of a Curl

Circle

Stem (Arc)

Base

Every curl, regardless of the chosen tool, has three components:

>> Base   >> Stem (Arc)   >> Circle

The base is the area between straight or curved partings within a shape, or the section of hair on which the roller, thermal iron or round brush is placed.

The **stem**, or **arc**, is the hair between the scalp and the first turn of the hair around the roller, thermal iron or round brush.

>> Determines the amount of movement of the section of hair
  ▪ Longer stems create more movement
  ▪ Shorter stems create less movement and more base strength (support)

The **circle** of a curl is the hair that is positioned around the roller, thermal iron or round brush.

>> Determines the size of the curl
>> Diameter of the tool you choose will determine the size of the circle

FINISHING PROCEDURES

The finishing procedures of a hair design are just as important as the setting procedures. The finishing phase is often referred to as the "comb-out." Here, you will blend areas of the design, create support, add volume, define the form and add finishing touches.

The finishing procedures that lead to predictable results are:
1. Relax
2. Dry Mold
3. Backcomb or Backbrush
4. Define the Form
5. Detail

| Relax | Dry Mold | Backcomb/Backbrush | Define the Form | Detail |

Regardless of the tools and methods used to set the hair, these finishing procedures are similar for many wet and thermal designs. Like setting, some of the finishing procedures may be combined or even omitted, depending on the desired results and how long the design is intended to last. For example, backcombing/backbrushing may be omitted for a more casual expression.

| Relax | Define the Form | Detail |

RELAX

Once the hair is dry, the set can be relaxed to collapse, integrate and blend the bases using cushion brush(es), a wide-tooth tail comb or your fingers.

DRY MOLD

Dry molding is performed on the surface of the hair to retrace and reinforce the established lines of the design.

Usually one or two cushion brushes are used to integrate the bases and soften the curl texture. Working within, and against, the set lines ensures thorough relaxing.

Relaxing with fingers is usually done to break up the surface texture and to piece out individual curls.

Usually performed with a cushion brush to retrace the lines of the set, following each movement with the other hand on top of the hair to control lengths with the heat of your palm.

BACKCOMB/BACKBRUSH

Backcombing and backbrushing are optional techniques used to increase height and controls the form in a hair design by creating a cushion or mesh at the base. They are most effective when the hair has been texturized, since the shorter lengths are directed down to the base, creating support for the longer lengths.

Backcomb

>> Backcombing is performed underneath the surface of the hair.

>> A small section of hair is held taut with one hand, while the other hand is used to direct the lengths with the comb toward the base.

>> The cushion created at the base expands the form and connects the bases for a more structured and controlled finish.

>> In some instances, a large-tooth comb can be used on the surface of the hair to lightly blend the bases and to create a detailed textured finish with an airy effect.

>> Backcombing is also called French lacing, teasing, ratting, matting and ruffing.

Backbrush

>> Backbrushing is performed on top of the strand to achieve a light, airy effect.

>> A small section of hair is held taut with one hand, while the other hand gently slides the brush from the ends toward the base.

>> The brush is turned outward at the base to carefully remove the hair from the brush.

>> The bristles of the brush are then used to pick up the next section and the backbrushing technique is repeated until the desired effect is achieved.

>> A wide-tooth tail comb can also be used on the surface for a more piecy result.

DEFINE THE FORM

Defining the form includes smoothing the surface of the hair, redefining the lines of the design and controlling the amount of desired volume.

DETAIL

Detailing is adding finishing touches, such as piecing or pleating the hair for additional texture and to personalize the form.

>> Opportunity to emphasize your client's personal style

>> Requires a light touch and a certain amount of restraint

>> Too much "detail" can overwhelm the integrity of the design, resulting in a fussy or overworked design

LESSONS LEARNED

>> The setting procedures used in hair design include:

1. **Distribute** – The direction the hair is combed or dispersed over the curve of the head; includes parallel and radial

2. **Mold**, or shape – Designing wet hair in straight or curved lines after the hair has been distributed to create a pattern

3. **Scale**, or section – Carving out shapes in the proper predetermined size and proportion to establish the lines of the design; straight shapes include rectangles, triangles and trapezoids; curvature shapes include circles, ovals and oblongs

4. **Part** – Lines that subdivide shapes or sections to help distribute and control the hair; include parallel, radial, horizontal, diagonal or vertical; used to create subsections, often referred to as bases; bases include rectangle, triangle, trapezoid and rhomboid

5. **Apply** – Setting the hair with a tool, such as a roller, thermal iron, round brush or pincurl

>> The finishing procedures used in hair design are:

1. **Relax** – Collapsing or integrating the bases using cushion brush(es), a wide-tooth tail comb or your fingers

2. **Dry Mold** – Retracing and reinforcing the lines of the design

3. **Backcomb/Backbrush** – Optional techniques used to increase height and control the form in a hair design by creating a cushion or mesh at the base

4. **Define the Form** – Smoothing the surface of the hair, redefining the lines of the design and controlling the amount of volume, especially if backcombing or backbrushing was performed

5. **Detail** – Adding finishing touches, such as piecing or pleating the hair to personalize the form

SALON CONNECTION

Finish What You *Set* Out To Do!

In the salon, you may be pressed for time, but taking shortcuts may prove regretful, not to mention unattractive. Taking the time to properly set and finish your client's hair can mean the difference between a satisfied and a not-so-satisfied client. Keep in mind that both setting and finishing procedures are equally important and support Aristotle's saying, "Well begun is half-done!" Setting the hair properly and keeping the end result in mind, regardless of the tools chosen, will enable you to finish the hair effortlessly and beautifully!

HAIR DESIGN
GUEST EXPERIENCE
107°.4 //

Think of a time you experienced great service, and not-so-great service, at a place of business—how did that make you feel?

INSPIRE //

Design skills and creativity are a must in our industry, but giving your client a positive personal experience keeps them coming back to you!

ACHIEVE //

Following this lesson on *Hair Design Guest Experience*, you'll be able to:

>> Summarize the service essentials related to hair design

>> Provide examples of infection control and safety guidelines for hair design services

FOCUS //

**HAIR DESIGN
GUEST EXPERIENCE**

Hair Design Service Essentials

Hair Design Infection Control and Safety

107ᶜ.4 | HAIR DESIGN GUEST EXPERIENCE

A key factor for a successful hair design service is clear communication. You can use photos and magazines to share ideas and confirm you and your client have the same vision. Concentrate on changes that can be made in the form, texture and direction of the design. If possible, show your client design finishes created on similar hair lengths to theirs.

It's also a good idea to teach your client some basic techniques for maintaining the hair design after leaving the salon, such as adding hairspray for support. Knowing some options they can do at home will increase the longevity and enjoyment of the hair design.

HAIR DESIGN SERVICE ESSENTIALS

To offer an exceptional hair design guest experience, pay attention to the following guidelines—from the initial greeting to the completion of the service.

CONNECT

>> Meet and greet the client with a firm handshake and pleasant tone of voice.

>> Communicate to build rapport and develop a relationship with the client.

CONSULT

>> Ask questions to discover client's needs, lifestyle and if additional services are desired.

>> Ask questions to determine the appropriate setting procedures.

  ▪ What is the occasion that brings you in for a hairstyle today?

  ▪ Did you bring a picture that resembles the style you would like?

  ▪ Would you like a softer or more structured finish?

  ▪ Do you prefer your hair to move toward your face or away from your face?

  ▪ Can you describe the type of curl you would like to achieve?

  ▪ Where would you like to see more or less fullness?

>> Ask questions to determine the finishing procedures required to achieve the desired results.

  ▪ Are there any products that you would like me to avoid using?

  ▪ Are you going for a more casual or formal look?

  ▪ Under what conditions does this design need to last?

  ▪ Can you describe the type of finish; is it soft and flowing or more strong to hold up to dancing?

  ▪ Would you like a smooth, sleek finish or an airy and piecy finish?

>> Analyze your client's face and body shape, physical features, hair and scalp.

>> Assess the facts and thoroughly think through your recommendations by visualizing the end result.

>> Organize and summarize your recommended solutions, products, and the price for today's service(s) as well as for future services.

>> Gain feedback from your client and obtain consent before proceeding with the service.

CREATE

>> Ensure your client's protection by using proper draping procedures.

>> Perform a scalp massage to relax the client while shampooing their hair.

>> Ensure client comfort during the service:

- Replace the towel with a neck strip.

- Replace the plastic cape with a cloth cape during the comb-out procedure.

>> Stay focused on delivering the hair design service to the best of your ability.

>> Produce a functional, predictable and pleasing result.

>> Personalize the hair design to add your signature touch.

>> Explain to your client the products you are using throughout the service, and why.

>> Allow the client to hold the product and to test it in their palm to become familiar with the scent and feel.

>> Teach your client how to perform at-home maintenance of the new hair design, if applicable.

COMPLETE

>> Request specific feedback from your client. Ask questions and look for verbal and nonverbal cues to determine your client's overall satisfaction.

>> Escort client to the retail area and show the products you used. Products may include shampoo and conditioner or styling and finishing products.

>> Recommend products to maintain the appearance and condition of your client's hair.

>> Invite your client to make a retail purchase for home care.

>> Prebook – Suggest a future appointment time for your client's next visit.

>> Offer sincere appreciation to your client for visiting the school or salon.

>> Complete client record for future visits; include recommended products.

COMMUNICATION GUIDELINES
Respond to common client cues in a way that encourages client trust and open communication.

CLIENT CUE	DESIGNER RESPONSE
"My scalp gets itchy when I use mousse to style my hair."	"Could you please explain to me how you're applying the mousse at home? One great way to apply mousse without touching the scalp is to put it between the bristles of a vent brush and brush it in. This not only avoids contact with the scalp but also helps distribute it much more evenly."
"What can I do to protect my hair from the heat of my curling iron?"	"I recommend a thermal protectant product. Thermal protectants come in a variety of forms, such as sprays, lotions and creams. They contain moisturizing additives that protect against heat from curling irons as well as blow dryers. In addition, these products often lend shine and style support. I think this one would be best for your hair."
"I always have trouble using hairspray. I get too much in one area and the rest of my hair doesn't hold."	"Make sure to check the instructions on the container, which most product companies provide. On average, hairspray should be held at least 10" to 12" (25 to 30 cm) away from the hair while spraying. This allows the product to be applied to a wider area, not in a concentrated area, which prevents over-saturation. Also, you can opt for an aerosol spray. It usually feels dryer and leaves the hair more workable after it has been applied."
"I really don't know what to do about the cowlick in the back of my head. The hair in that area just does whatever it wants."	"I took your cowlick into consideration when I designed your hair today. Let me show you what I did when I styled your hair. I'll turn you with your back toward the mirror and let you hold this mirror so you can watch while I share my techniques with you. With a bit of practice I am sure this cowlick won't give you any more problems."
"I really wouldn't mind my curly hair if I just knew what to do with it. It always seems to get frizzy."	"There are a few products you can use to make your curls look great. While your hair is still wet, apply a curl cream that contains moisture. As you apply it, twist individual strands of hair and either diffuse your hair or let it air dry in this formation. Once it's dry, distribute a silicone-based product during this final stage of finishing, using your fingers. I can show you these products and how to use them."
"I can't style my hair anymore, so I was hoping you have a solution that wouldn't require a lot of work for me."	"I would be more than happy to. If you want to avoid chemicals, come in once or twice a week and I'll set your hair to achieve a longer-lasting style. I can also teach you how to maintain it between visits. Or, if you like, I can perm your hair, which would give additional support to salon finishes. At home you just shampoo it and let it dry. Do any of these options sound good to you?"
"I just got this new haircut, but have no idea how to style it. Can you give me some hints?"	"Absolutely. One way is to blow dry it straight with a bit of curl on the ends, I can show you how you can do that with a vent brush and a round brush. For a more dressed finish, I'll show you how to use a curling iron to add a stronger curl pattern. Additionally, there are a few products that I can show you to achieve different looks, from smooth and sleek to soft and flowing."

HAIR DESIGN INFECTION CONTROL AND SAFETY

It is your responsibility as a professional to protect your client by following infection control and safety guidelines with any and all services you provide.

Cleaning is a process of removing dirt, debris and potential pathogens to aid in slowing the growth of pathogens. Cleaning is performed prior to disinfection procedures.

Disinfection methods kill certain pathogens (bacteria, viruses and fungi) with the exception of spores. Disinfectants are available in varied forms, including concentrate, liquid, spray or wipes that are approved EPA-registered disinfectants available for use in the salon industry. Immersion, and the use of disinfecting spray or wipes are the common practices when it comes to disinfecting tools, multi-use supplies and equipment in the salon. Be sure to follow the manufacturer's directions for mixing disinfecting solutions and contact time if applicable.

CLEANING AND DISINFECTION GUIDELINES

Keep in mind that only nonporous tools, supplies and equipment can be disinfected. All single-use items must be discarded after each use. Always follow your area's regulatory guidelines.

TOOLS, SUPPLIES AND EQUIPMENT	CLEANING GUIDELINES	DISINFECTION GUIDELINES
Combs/Brushes	» Remove hair and debris. » Preclean with soap and water.	» Immerse in an approved EPA-registered disinfectant solution.
Rollers (nonporous)	» Remove hair and debris. » Preclean with soap and water.	» Immerse in an approved EPA-registered disinfectant solution.
Hand-Held Dryer	» Clean vent with a toothbrush or a damp cloth to remove buildup as often as necessary. » If dryer has a filter, wash with soap and water, allow to dry thoroughly.	» Use an approved EPA-registered disinfectant wipe or spray as directed.
Thermal Irons/Combs	» Clean cooled iron barrel/pressing combs with a spray cleaner to remove buildup. » Heavily soiled irons/pressing combs may be cleaned with a fine steel wool first.	» Use an approved EPA-registered disinfectant wipe or spray as directed.
Cape (plastic and cloth)	» Remove hair from cape. » Wash in washing machine with soap after each use.	» Some regulatory agencies may require use of an approved EPA-registered disinfectant.
Neck Strip	» Single-use item; must be discarded.	» Cannot be disinfected.

Store disinfected tools and multi-use supplies in a clean, dry, covered container or cabinet.

 **Alert!** If tools, multi-use supplies or equipment have come in contact with blood or body fluids, the following disinfection procedures must take place:

 Use an approved EPA-registered hospital disinfectant according to manufacturer's directions and as required by your area's regulatory agency.

CARE AND SAFETY

Follow infection control procedures for personal care and client safety guidelines before and during the hairstyling service to ensure your safety and the client's, while also contributing to the salon care.

Personal Care		Client Care Prior to the Service	
	» Clean and disinfect tools appropriately.		» Check the scalp for any diseases or disorders. If any are evident, refer the client to a physician and do not proceed with the service.
» Check that your personal standards of health and hygiene minimize the spread of infection.	» Wear single-use gloves as required.	» Protect the client's skin and clothing from water with a freshly laundered towel and a freshly laundered plastic or waterproof cape.	» Replace towel with neck strip after shampoo.
» Wash hands and dry thoroughly with a single-use towel.	» Refer to your area's regulatory agency for proper mixing/handling of disinfectant solutions.	» Be sure the cape stays in place and the client's arms are underneath the cape.	» Ensure that the client does not have sensitivities to any styling products, such as mousse or gel that will be used during the service.
» Disinfect workstation.	» Minimize fatigue by maintaining good posture during the service.		

 SALONCONNECTION

Nonverbal Communication – Ouch! That's Too Hot!

Be alert for any nonverbal cues your client may be giving you. Watch their face for grimaces, or signs of discomfort such as pulling their head away from you as you are pulling their hair with the brush, or because the heat from the blow dryer is too hot for their scalp. Ask your client frequently if they are comfortable throughout the service.

Client Care During the Service		Salon Care	

	» Perform thermal iron procedures only on dry hair.		» Promote a professional image by ensuring your workstation is clean and tidy throughout the service.
» Perform first-aid procedures if a burn occurs on you or your client.	» Be careful when removing tools and supplies from client's hair during the setting process.	» Follow health and safety guidelines including cleaning and disinfecting procedures.	» Ensure equipment, including the salon chair and shampoo chair, is clean and disinfected.
» Avoid pressing hair too often—hair may suffer progressive hair breakage.	» Periodically ask your client if the heat from the blow dryer is too hot for their scalp.	» Check the air-intake area on the blow dryer to ensure it is free from debris.	» Disinfect all tools after each use. Always use disinfected combs, rollers and brushes for each client.
» Before placing a client under a hood dryer, check that no metal pins or clips are touching the skin. ▪ Check frequently on client to ensure the dryer temperature is comfortable	» Use lower temperatures and shorter contact time on hair that has been chemically treated, altered (lightened) or shows signs of mechanical damage, or recommend a wet set.	» Ensure electrical cords are properly positioned to avoid accidental falls.	» Ensure electrical equipment, plugs and cables are in good condition and remember to turn off after use.
» Check the temperature of stove-heated pressing combs and thermal irons, by testing on a piece of white paper towel.	» Avoid having the teeth of the hot pressing comb come in contact with the client's scalp.	» Report malfunctioning furniture/equipment to manager.	» Clean/mop water spillage from floor to avoid accidental falls.
» Avoid using excess tension on the hair and scalp when styling.	» Store soiled towels in a dry, covered receptacle until laundered.		
» Complete the client record noting contraindications.	» Work carefully around non-removable jewelry/ piercings.		
» Test the temperature of thermal irons or pressing combs before applying to client's hair. ▪ Use thermal-protectant products and avoid high temperatures ▪ Protect the client's skin by positioning a hard-rubber or nonflammable comb underneath the iron			

DISCOVER**MORE**

White-Glove Test
Have you ever been to a 5-star hotel or restaurant? If so, at first glance you noticed how clean it was—and you knew they would pass a "white glove test." Chances are, these businesses pride themselves on cleanliness from floor to ceiling and everything in between. They pay close attention to the smallest detail so guests can enjoy themselves—dirt free. In the salon, it's your responsibility to keep your tools and equipment clean and disinfected. Paying attention to details, such as cleaning the barrel of your curling iron so it looks brand-new each time you use it, or cleaning the debris from the vent of your blow dryer, do not go unnoticed by your clients. And no one wants a comb or brush with someone else's hair put on their head— make sure your tools are ALWAYS hair-free. It is your responsibility to make your clients feel like they are walking into a 5-star salon. Research 5-star businesses to see what guests are saying about "cleanliness." Then make a list of the comments to use as a reminder as you try to create your own 5-star atmosphere.

LESSONS LEARNED

The service essentials related to hair design can be summarized as follows:

>> Connect – Meet and greet client to build rapport.

>> Consult – Ask questions to discover client needs and to determine setting and finishing procedures; analyze client face, body shape, physical features, hair and scalp; assess the facts and think through recommendations; organize and summarize recommended solutions and gain feedback for consent to move forward.

>> Create – Ensure client safety and comfort; stay focused to deliver the best service; produce a functional, predictable result and teach about product usage.

>> Complete – Request specific feedback; recommend products you used; suggest future appointment times; complete client record.

Infection control and safety guidelines must be followed throughout a hair design service to ensure your safety and the safety of the clients and the salon. Disinfectants are available in varied forms, including concentrate, liquid, spray or wipes that have EPA approval for use in the salon industry. Be guided by your area's regulatory agency for proper cleaning and disinfection guidelines.

By following the four Service Essentials and following proper infection control and safety guidelines, you will be able to create a pleasant salon experience and build a loyal clientele.

EXPLORE //

Can you think of
things that come in
threes or slogans that
include three words?

107ᶜ.5 //
HAIR DESIGN SERVICE

INSPIRE //

Preparation, Procedure, Completion:
Focusing on these three areas will lead to
a perfect hair design service.

ACHIEVE //

Following this lesson on *Hair Design Service*, you'll be able to:

>> Provide examples of guidelines to ensure client comfort and
satisfaction when performing a hair design service

>> Describe the three areas of a hair design service

FOCUS //

HAIR DESIGN SERVICE

Hair Design Client Guidelines

Hair Design Service Overview

Hair Design Rubrics

T 107ᶜ.5 | HAIR DESIGN SERVICE

his lesson is a culmination of everything you've learned about hair design theory, tools, skills and guest relations; it's where you apply your knowledge before, during and after the hair design service to ensure client safety and satisfaction.

HAIR DESIGN CLIENT GUIDELINES

Combining your experience with predictable setting and finishing procedures will lead to exceptional results and a pleasant service experience for your client. To ensure your client's comfort and satisfaction during a hair design service, keep the following setting and finishing guidelines in mind.

SETTING

Distribute/Mold

>> Face client toward mirror and discuss the direction of the design.

>> Monitor the temperature of the heat to ensure client comfort when air forming.

>> Explain your choice of setting products and how the client might use them at home.

Scale/Part/Apply

>> Avoid pulling the hair when scaling each individual section.

>> Avoid scratching the client's scalp with the tail comb.

>> Ensure the tip of the comb is smooth and not irritating the client's scalp.

>> Protect the client's scalp from thermal irons by positioning a hard-rubber or nonflammable heat-resistant comb under the irons.

>> Give your client tips and hints on how they can apply some of your setting techniques at home.

>> Explain the tools you are using and how the client can adapt your techniques at home.

FINISHING

Relax/Dry Mold

» Be sure to use brushes that are easy on the scalp and don't cause discomfort when relaxing.

» Avoid sharp or broken teeth and heavy pressure.

» When using your fingers, be sure your nails are not sharp or split to avoid scratching the scalp and pulling the hair.

Backbrush/Backcomb (Optional)

» Avoid excessive tension and pulling the hair.

» Avoid matting the hair at the scalp.

» Teach the client how to remove backbrushed/ backcombed hair from ends to base.

Define and Detail Form

» Control the amount of volume when defining the form according to the client's desires, and check for overall balance.

» Add detailed finishing touches to personalize the design.

» Give client a hand-held mirror so they may view all areas of the design; with their approval, make any necessary adjustments.

» Remember to teach client how to use finishing products to maintain the design for that special occasion or in-between.

HAIR DESIGN SERVICE OVERVIEW

The Hair Design Service Overview identifies the three areas of every hair design service:

>> The Hair Design Preparation provides a brief overview of the steps to follow *before* you actually begin the hair design.

>> The Hair Design Procedure provides an overview of the setting and finishing procedures that you will use *during* the hair design to ensure predictable results.

>> The Hair Design Completion provides an overview of the steps to follow *after* performing the hair design to ensure guest satisfaction.

SALON**CONNECTION**

Ready – Set – Finish!
Hairstyles can be one of the most creative ways clients express themselves. It's up to you to teach your client how to create various finishes to suit their ever-changing and ever-evolving style. Whether it's fingerstyling techniques to create a funky finish, glamming it up for a wedding or providing a classic finish for a weekly service, clients should know how to reproduce or maintain the finish you achieve in the salon. By practicing various services and following a set of guidelines, you will be ready to meet and exceed your client's expectations!

Service Essentials: The Four Cs

The hair design procedures include attention to the Four Cs.

1. **Connect**
   Establishes rapport and builds credibility with each client

2. **Consult**
   Analyzes client wants and needs, visualizes the end result, organizes the plan for follow-through and obtains client agreement

3. **Create**
   Produces functional, predictable and pleasing results

4. **Complete**
   Reviews the service experience and client satisfaction, offers product recommendations, expresses appreciation and provides follow-up

DISCOVER**MORE**

Interview the Best

Have you ever wondered how someone became the "best" or most sought-after in their profession? Many successful professionals will tell you it's because they practiced, practiced, practiced their skill until it became second nature to them. In other words, there are no shortcuts to becoming the best. British economist Ernst Friedrich "Fritz" Schumacher once said, "An ounce of practice is generally worth more than a ton of theory." Ask your mentors, seek out the best or search the Internet to discover how some of the industry's best achieved success in their field. Then, ask yourself what you will do to set yourself apart from the rest.

WET-SETTING AND FINISHING SERVICE OVERVIEW

HAIR DESIGN PREPARATION	>> Clean and disinfect workstation. >> Arrange disinfected hair design tools and supplies, including combs, brushes, rollers, picks, clips, spray bottle and cape. >> Wash hands. >> Perform analysis of hair and scalp. >> Ask client to remove jewelry; store in a secure place.

HAIR DESIGN PROCEDURE	>> Drape client for the service.
	>> Shampoo and condition client's hair.
	>> Replace client's towel with a neck strip.
	
	>> Perform the wet-setting procedures to achieve desired results.
	>> Apply the appropriate setting product evenly throughout the hair.
	1. **Distribute** the hair into the desired direction in relation to the client's face shape.
	2. **Mold** the hair into straight and/or curved lines (parallel/radial).
	3. **Scale** (section) the hair into straight and/or curvature shapes and in the proper predetermined size and proportion (rectangles, triangles, circles, ovals, oblongs).
	4. **Part** to create bases or subsections or to control the hair as needed.
	    ■ Partings (horizontal, vertical, diagonal).
	    ■ Bases (rectangle, triangle, trapezoid, rhomboid).
	5. **Apply** base controls to achieve the desired degree of volume and/or indentation (overdirected, on base, underdirected, half-off base, off base).
	    ■ Wrap hair evenly and smoothly around roller.
	    ■ Ribbon hair smoothly when forming pincurls.
	    ■ Secure rollers and/or pincurls appropriately (picks/clips).
	>> Place client under a hood dryer and monitor their comfort.
	>> Allow the hair to cool before removing tools.
	
	>> Perform the finishing procedures as applicable:
	1. **Relax** the hair to blend and integrate the bases and soften the curl texture.
	2. **Dry mold** the hair to reinforce the established lines of the design.
	3. **Backbrush/backcomb** (optional) to create volume and indentation, expand the design's shape and/or connect shapes within the design.
	4. **Define the form** to achieve the desired finish.
	5. **Detail** the hair to add finishing touches and/or to personalize the design.
	>> Check for overall balance.

HAIR DESIGN COMPLETION	>> Reinforce client's satisfaction with overall salon experience. >> Make professional product recommendations. >> Prebook client's next appointment. >> End client's visit with warm and personal goodbye. >> Discard single-use supplies; disinfect tools and multi-use supplies; disinfect workstation and arrange in proper order. >> Complete client record. >> Wash hands.

HAIR DESIGN RUBRICS

A performance rubric is a document that identifies defined criteria at which levels of performance can be measured objectively. The following are rubrics that your instructor might choose to use for scoring. Each hair design rubric is divided into three main areas—Preparation, Procedure and Completion. Each area is further divided into step-by-step procedures that will ensure client safety and satisfaction.

WET-SETTING AND FINISHING RUBRIC

Allotted Time: 1 Hour, 30 Minutes

Student Name: _____ ID Number: _____

Instructor: _____ Date: _____ Start Time: _____ End Time: _____

WET-SETTING (Live Model) – *Each scoring item is marked with either a "Yes" or "No." Each "Yes" counts for one point. Total number of points attainable is 35.*

CRITERIA	YES	NO	INSTRUCTOR ASSESSMENT
PREPARATION: *Did student...*			
1. Set up workstation with properly labeled supplies?	☐	☐	
2. Place disinfected tools and supplies at a visibly clean workstation?	☐	☐	
3. Wash their hands?	☐	☐	
Connect: Did student...			
4. Meet and greet client with a welcoming smile and pleasant tone?	☐	☐	
5. Communicate to build rapport and develop a relationship with client?	☐	☐	
6. Refer to client by name throughout service?	☐	☐	
Consult: Did student...			
7. Ask questions to discover client's wants and needs?	☐	☐	
8. Analyze client's hair and scalp and check for any contraindications?	☐	☐	
9. Gain feedback and consent from client before proceeding?	☐	☐	
PROCEDURE: *Did student...*			
10. Properly drape client and prepare for service?	☐	☐	
11. Ensure client protection and comfort by maintaining cape on outside of chair at all times?	☐	☐	
12. Carry out appropriate shampoo and condition procedures?	☐	☐	
13. Use products economically?	☐	☐	
Create: Did student...			
14. Apply appropriate setting product evenly throughout the hair?	☐	☐	
15. Distribute and mold the hair in straight and/or curved lines to establish the lines of the design?	☐	☐	
16. Scale out shapes in the predetermined size and proportion?	☐	☐	
17. Part and apply the correct base controls to achieve the desired volume and/or indentation?	☐	☐	
18. Place client under a hood dryer and monitor their comfort?	☐	☐	
19. Allow the set to dry and cool completely before removing tools?	☐	☐	
20. Relax the set to blend, integrate the bases and soften the curl texture?	☐	☐	
21. Dry mold the hair following the lines of the set?	☐	☐	
22. Backbrush/backcomb (optional) to increase height and control the form?	☐	☐	
23. Define and detail the form to achieve the desired finish?	☐	☐	
24. Check for balance in the final design?	☐	☐	
25. Teach client to use products to maintain the design at home?	☐	☐	
26. Practice infection control procedures and safety guidelines throughout service?	☐	☐	
COMPLETION *(Complete): Did student...*			
27. Ask questions and look for verbal and nonverbal cues to determine client's level of satisfaction?	☐	☐	
28. Make professional product recommendations?	☐	☐	
29. Ask client to make a future appointment?	☐	☐	
30. End client's visit with a warm and personal goodbye?	☐	☐	
31. Discard single-use supplies?	☐	☐	
32. Disinfect tools and multi-use supplies; disinfect workstation and arrange in proper order?	☐	☐	
33. Complete service within scheduled time?	☐	☐	
34. Complete client record?	☐	☐	
35. Wash their hands following service?	☐	☐	

COMMENTS: _____ TOTAL POINTS = _____ ÷ 35 = _____ %

FINGERWAVES AND PINCURLS SERVICE OVERVIEW

HAIR DESIGN PREPARATION	>> Clean and disinfect workstation. >> Arrange disinfected hair design tools and supplies, including combs, brushes, clips, spray bottle and cape. >> Wash hands. >> Perform analysis of hair and scalp. >> Ask client to remove jewelry; store in a secure place.

HAIR DESIGN PROCEDURE	>> Drape client for the service.
	>> Shampoo and condition client's hair.
	>> Replace client's towel with a neck strip.
	>> Perform the wet-setting procedures to achieve desired results.
	>> Apply appropriate product evenly throughout the hair.
	1-2. **Distribute** and **mold** alternating oblong shapes:
	    ▪ Distribute 1st direction toward convex end.
	    ▪ Distribute 2nd direction toward concave end.
	    ▪ Mold parallel curved "C" lines.
	    ▪ Form ridge beginning at concave end.
	    ▪ Strive for equally spaced alternating oblongs.
	3. **Scale** oblong to prepare for flat pincurls.
	4-5. **Part** and **apply** flat pincurls without disturbing ridge:
	    ▪ Begin at concave end and create a curved parting in 2nd direction
	    ▪ Ribbon the hair strand smoothly to form the pincurl circle.
	    ▪ Form pincurl without disturbing molded shape.
	    ▪ Apply flat pincurl in front of base and secure in 2nd direction.
	    ▪ Securing pincurls with clips.
	    ▪ Repeat procedures for pincurls to complete the design.
	>> Place client under a hood dryer and monitor their comfort.
	>> Allow the hair to cool before removing tools.
	>> Perform the finishing procedures as applicable:
	1. **Relax** the hair to blend and integrate the bases and soften the curl texture.
	2. **Dry mold** the hair to reinforce the established lines of the design.
	3. **Backbrush/backcomb** (optional) to create volume and indentation, expand the design's shape and/or connect shapes within the design.
	4. **Define the form** to refine and achieve the desired finish.
	5. **Detail** the hair to add finishing touches and/or to personalize the design.
	>> Check for overall balance.

HAIR DESIGN COMPLETION	>> Reinforce client's satisfaction with overall salon experience. >> Make professional product recommendations. >> Prebook client's next appointment. >> End client's visit with warm and personal goodbye. >> Discard single-use supplies; disinfect tools and multi-use supplies; disinfect workstation and arrange in proper order. >> Complete client record. >> Wash hands.

FINGERWAVES AND PINCURLS RUBRIC

Student Name: _____ ID Number: _____

Instructor: _____ Date: _____ Start Time: _____ End Time: _____

FINGERWAVES and PINCURLS (Live Model) – *Each scoring item is marked with either a "Yes" or "No." Each "Yes" counts for one point. Total number of points attainable is 34.*

CRITERIA	YES	NO	INSTRUCTOR ASSESSMENT
PREPARATION: *Did student...*			
1. Set up workstation with properly labeled supplies?	☐	☐	
2. Place disinfected tools and supplies at a visibly clean workstation?	☐	☐	
3. Wash their hands?	☐	☐	
Connect: Did student...			
4. Meet and greet client with a welcoming smile and pleasant tone?	☐	☐	
5. Communicate to build rapport and develop a relationship with client?	☐	☐	
6. Refer to client by name throughout service?	☐	☐	
Consult: Did student...			
7. Ask questions to discover client's wants and needs?	☐	☐	
8. Analyze client's hair and scalp and check for any contraindications?	☐	☐	
9. Gain feedback and consent from client before proceeding?	☐	☐	
PROCEDURE: *Did student...*			
10. Properly drape client and prepare for service?	☐	☐	
11. Ensure client protection and comfort by maintaining cape on outside of chair at all times?	☐	☐	
12. Carry out appropriate shampoo and condition procedures?	☐	☐	
13. Use products economically?	☐	☐	
Create: Did student...			
14. Apply appropriate product evenly throughout the hair?	☐	☐	
15. Distribute the hair smoothly in the direction of the intended design?	☐	☐	
16. Mold parallel "C" lines to establish the first oblong?	☐	☐	
17. Create ridge beginning at concave end and working toward convex end?	☐	☐	
18. Part and apply flat pincurls beginning at the concave end without disturbing ridge?	☐	☐	
19. Create a well-balanced fingerwave design with defined ridges finished with pincurls?	☐	☐	
20. Place client under a hood dryer and monitor their comfort?	☐	☐	
21. Allow the set to dry and cool completely before removing tools?	☐	☐	
22. Dry mold the hair to reinforce the lines of the design?	☐	☐	
23. Define and detail the form to blend the waves with the pincurls?	☐	☐	
24. Teach client to use products to maintain the design at home?	☐	☐	
25. Practice infection control procedures and safety guidelines throughout service?	☐	☐	
COMPLETION (Complete): *Did student...*			
26. Ask questions and look for verbal and nonverbal cues to determine client's level of satisfaction?	☐	☐	
27. Make professional product recommendations?	☐	☐	
28. Ask client to make a future appointment?	☐	☐	
29. End client's visit with a warm and personal goodbye?	☐	☐	
30. Discard single-use supplies?	☐	☐	
31. Disinfect tools and multi-use supplies; disinfect workstation and arrange in proper order?	☐	☐	
32. Complete service within scheduled time?	☐	☐	
33. Complete client record?	☐	☐	
34. Wash their hands following service?	☐	☐	

COMMENTS: _____ TOTAL POINTS = _____ ÷ 34 = _____ %

AIR FORMING SERVICE OVERVIEW

HAIR DESIGN PREPARATION	
	>> Clean and disinfect workstation.
	>> Arrange disinfected hair design tools and supplies, including combs, brushes, clips, blow dryer with attachments and cape.
	>> Wash hands.
	>> Perform analysis of hair and scalp.
	>> Ask client to remove jewelry; store in a secure place.

HAIR DESIGN PROCEDURE

>> Drape client for the service.
>> Shampoo and condition client's hair.
>> Replace client's towel with a neck strip.

>> Perform thermal setting procedures to achieve desired results.
>> Apply thermal protectant evenly throughout hair.
>> Remove excess moisture from hair using a blow dryer, vent brush and/or your fingers.

1-2. **Distribute** and **mold** the hair simultaneously to establish the directional pattern of the design before and/or during air forming.
- Distribute and mold the hair into straight or curved lines, using parallel and/or radial distribution.
- Control the form and the lines of the design as the molded directions are air formed.

3-5. **Scale** (section), **part** and **apply** the proper base controls using the appropriate tools (brushes/combs) in a repetitive motion to control the amount of volume and/or indentation and direction within the design, while blending the bases and shapes.
- Scale the hair into straight and/or curvature shapes in the proper predetermined size and proportion (rectangles, triangles, circles, ovals, oblongs).
- Part to create bases or subsections, or to control the hair as needed.
  - Partings (horizontal, vertical, diagonal).
  - Bases (rectangle, triangle, trapezoid, rhomboid).
- Apply base controls (overdirected, on base, underdirected, half-off base, off base).

>> Choose appropriate tools (brushes/combs).
>> Air form the base, midstrand and ends.
>> Direct airflow in the direction of the cuticle.
>> Allow curls/hair to cool and set before applying finishing techniques.

>> Perform finishing procedures as applicable:

1-2. **Relax** and **dry mold** the hair to reinforce the established lines of the design.
3. **Backbrush/backcomb** (optional) to create volume and indentation, expand the design's shape and/or connect shapes within the design.
4. **Define the form** to refine and achieve the desired finish.
5. **Detail** the hair to add your finishing touches and/or to personalize the design.
>> Check for overall balance.

HAIR DESIGN COMPLETION

>> Reinforce client's satisfaction with overall salon experience.
>> Make professional product recommendations.
>> Prebook client's next appointment.
>> End client's visit with warm and personal goodbye.
>> Discard single-use supplies; disinfect tools and multi-use supplies; disinfect workstation and arrange in proper order.
>> Complete client record.
>> Wash hands.

AIR FORMING RUBRIC

Allotted Time: 30 Minutes

Student Name: _____ _____ ID Number: _____

Instructor: _____ Date: _____ Start Time: _____ End Time: _____

AIR FORMING (Live Model) – *Each scoring item is marked with either a "Yes" or "No." Each "Yes" counts for one point. Total number of points attainable is 34.*

CRITERIA	YES	NO	INSTRUCTOR ASSESSMENT
PREPARATION: *Did student...*			
1. Set up workstation with properly labeled supplies?	☐	☐	
2. Place disinfected tools and supplies at a visibly clean workstation?	☐	☐	
3. Wash their hands?	☐	☐	
Connect: Did student...			
4. Meet and greet client with a welcoming smile and pleasant tone?	☐	☐	
5. Communicate to build rapport and develop a relationship with client?	☐	☐	
6. Refer to client by name throughout service?	☐	☐	
Consult: Did student...			
7. Ask questions to discover client's wants and needs?	☐	☐	
8. Analyze client's hair and scalp and check for any contraindications?	☐	☐	
9. Gain feedback and consent from client before proceeding?	☐	☐	
PROCEDURE: *Did student...*			
10. Properly drape client and prepare for service?	☐	☐	
11. Ensure client protection and comfort by maintaining cape on outside of chair at all times?	☐	☐	
12. Carry out appropriate shampoo and condition procedures?	☐	☐	
13. Use products economically?	☐	☐	
Create: Did student...			
14. Apply thermal protectant product evenly through the hair?	☐	☐	
15. Remove excess moisture from hair?	☐	☐	
16. Distribute and mold hair simultaneously while air forming the lines of the design?	☐	☐	
17. Scale, part and apply the correct base controls to achieve volume and/or indentation?	☐	☐	
18. Direct the airflow in the direction of the cuticle, dry base, midstrand and ends?	☐	☐	
19. Monitor the temperature of the heat to ensure client comfort?	☐	☐	
20. Choose the appropriate air forming tools to achieve the desired results?	☐	☐	
21. Backbrush/backcomb (optional) to increase height and control the form?	☐	☐	
22. Define and detail the form to achieve the desired finish?	☐	☐	
23. Check for balance in the final design?	☐	☐	
24. Teach client to use products to maintain the design at home?	☐	☐	
25. Practice infection control procedures and safety guidelines throughout service?	☐	☐	
COMPLETION (Complete): *Did student...*			
26. Ask questions and look for verbal and nonverbal cues to determine client's level of satisfaction?	☐	☐	
27. Make professional product recommendations?	☐	☐	
28. Ask client to make a future appointment?	☐	☐	
29. End client's visit with a warm and personal goodbye?	☐	☐	
30. Discard single-use supplies?	☐	☐	
31. Disinfect tools and multi-use supplies; disinfect workstation and arrange in proper order?	☐	☐	
32. Complete service within scheduled time?	☐	☐	
33. Complete client record?	☐	☐	
34. Wash their hands following service?	☐	☐	

COMMENTS: _____ TOTAL POINTS = _____ ÷ 34 = _____ %

CURLING IRON SERVICE OVERVIEW

HAIR DESIGN PREPARATION	>> Clean and disinfect workstation. >> Arrange disinfected hair design tools and supplies, including combs, brushes, clips, curling iron and cape. >> Wash hands. >> Perform analysis of hair and scalp. >> Ask client to remove jewelry; store in a secure place.

HAIR DESIGN PROCEDURE	>> Drape client for the service.
	>> Shampoo and condition client's hair.
	>> Replace client's towel with a neck strip.
	>> Perform the appropriate thermal setting procedures to achieve desired results.
	>> Apply thermal protectant evenly throughout hair.
	>> Remove excess moisture from hair using a blow dryer, vent brush and/or your fingers.
	1-3. **Distribute**, **mold** and **scale** the hair simultaneously to establish the directional pattern of the design before and/or during air forming.
	   ▪ Air form the hair using the pre-determined base controls for the curling iron set.
	   ▪ Choose the appropriate brush(es) to establish the base direction and/or to air form volume and indentation.
	   ▪ Dry the hair completely before proceeding to the curling iron techniques.
	4-5. **Part** and **apply** curling iron procedures:
	   ▪ Test temperature of curling iron prior to applying it to hair.
	   ▪ Part to create bases or subsections, or to control the hair (horizontal, vertical, diagonal).
	   ▪ Bases (rectangle, triangle, trapezoid, rhomboid).
	   ▪ Base controls to achieve the desired degree of volume and/or indentation (overdirected, on base, underdirected, half-off base, off base).
	>> Choose the appropriate curling iron diameter(s) to achieve desired results.
	>> Adjust temperature of curling iron based on texture, density and porosity of hair.
	>> Feed ends of the hair all the way through the curling iron evenly to avoid crimped "fishhook" ends.
	>> Protect the scalp with a hard-rubber or nonflammable comb underneath the iron.
	>> Allow curls/hair to cool and set before applying finishing techniques.
	>> Perform finishing procedures as applicable:
	1-2. **Relax** and **dry mold** the hair to reinforce the established lines of the design.
	3. **Backbrush/backcomb** (optional) to create volume and indentation, expand the design's shape and/or connect shapes within the design.
	4. **Define the form** to refine and achieve the desired finish.
	5. **Detail** the hair to add your finishing touches and/or to personalize the design.
	>> Check for overall balance.

HAIR DESIGN COMPLETION	>> Reinforce client's satisfaction with overall salon experience. >> Make professional product recommendations. >> Prebook client's next appointment. >> End client's visit with warm and personal goodbye. >> Discard single-use supplies; disinfect tools and multi-use supplies; disinfect workstation and arrange in proper order. >> Complete client record. >> Wash hands.

CURLING IRON RUBRIC

Allotted Time: 45 Minutes

Student Name: _____ ID Number: _____

Instructor: _____ Date: _____ Start Time: _____ End Time: _____

CURLING IRON (Live Model) – *Each scoring item is marked with either a "Yes" or "No." Each "Yes" counts for one point. Total number of points attainable is 35.*

CRITERIA	YES	NO	INSTRUCTOR ASSESSMENT
PREPARATION: *Did student...*			
1. Set up workstation with properly labeled supplies?	☐	☐	
2. Place disinfected tools and supplies at a visibly clean workstation?	☐	☐	
3. Wash their hands?	☐	☐	
Connect: Did student...			
4. Meet and greet client with a welcoming smile and pleasant tone?	☐	☐	
5. Communicate to build rapport and develop a relationship with client?	☐	☐	
6. Refer to client by name throughout service?	☐	☐	
Consult: Did student...			
7. Ask questions to discover client's wants and needs?	☐	☐	
8. Analyze client's hair and scalp and check for any contraindications?	☐	☐	
9. Gain feedback and consent from client before proceeding?	☐	☐	
PROCEDURE: *Did student...*			
10. Properly drape client and prepare for service?	☐	☐	
11. Ensure client protection and comfort by maintaining cape on outside of chair at all times?	☐	☐	
12. Carry out appropriate shampoo and condition procedures?	☐	☐	
13. Apply product evenly through the hair?	☐	☐	
Create: Did student...			
14. Apply thermal protectant product evenly through the hair?	☐	☐	
15. Remove excess moisture from hair?	☐	☐	
16. Air form the hair to establish base direction, volume and/or indentation?	☐	☐	
17. Test temperature of iron prior to applying it to hair?	☐	☐	
18. Part and apply base controls to achieve volume and/or indentation with the curling iron?	☐	☐	
19. Feed ends of the hair all the way through the curling iron evenly to avoid crimped "fishhook" ends?	☐	☐	
20. Protect the scalp with a hard-rubber or nonflammable comb underneath the iron?	☐	☐	
21. Relax the set to blend, integrate the bases and soften the curl texture?	☐	☐	
22. Backbrush/backcomb (optional) to increase height and control the form?	☐	☐	
23. Define and detail the form to achieve the desired finish?	☐	☐	
24. Check for balance in the final design?	☐	☐	
25. Teach client to use products to maintain the design at home?	☐	☐	
26. Practice infection control procedures and safety guidelines throughout service?	☐	☐	
COMPLETION (Complete): *Did student...*			
27. Ask questions and look for verbal and nonverbal cues to determine client's level of satisfaction?	☐	☐	
28. Make professional product recommendations?	☐	☐	
29. Ask client to make a future appointment?	☐	☐	
30. End client's visit with a warm and personal goodbye?	☐	☐	
31. Discard single-use supplies?	☐	☐	
32. Disinfect tools and multi-use supplies; disinfect workstation and arrange in proper order?	☐	☐	
33. Complete service within scheduled time?	☐	☐	
34. Complete client record?	☐	☐	
35. Wash their hands following service?	☐	☐	

COMMENTS: _____ TOTAL POINTS = _____ ÷ 35 = _____ %

PRESS AND CURL SERVICE OVERVIEW

HAIR DESIGN PREPARATION	>> Clean and disinfect workstation. >> Arrange disinfected hair design tools and supplies including combs, brushes, pressing combs, stove, marcel irons and cape. >> Wash hands. >> Perform analysis of hair and scalp. >> Ask client to remove jewelry; store in a secure place.
HAIR DESIGN PROCEDURE	>> Drape client for the service. >> Detangle hair from ends to base >> Shampoo and condition client's hair. >> Replace client's towel with a neck strip. >> Detangle hair from ends to base. >> Perform the appropriate thermal setting procedures to achieve desired results. >> Apply thermal protectant evenly throughout hair. >> Remove excess moisture from hair using a blow dryer, vent brush and/or your fingers. >> Section the hair for control throughout the service. >> Distribute and air form hair straight in the direction of the intended design using appropriate brush(es). >> **Part** and **apply** pressing comb procedures: ▪ Test the temperature of the pressing comb on white paper towel prior to applying it to the hair. ▪ Part hair according to the density and texture of hair (horizontal, vertical and diagonal). ▪ Apply appropriate pressing technique (soft press, hard press). ▪ Press hair using the spine of the pressing comb. ▪ Press the hairline away from the face to achieve a smooth finish. >> **Part** and **apply** marcel iron procedures: ▪ Test temperature of marcel iron on white paper towel prior to applying it to the hair. ▪ Part to create bases or subsections, or to control the hair (horizontal, vertical and diagonal). ▪ Partings taken according to density of hair and diameter of marcel iron. ▪ Bases (rectangle, triangle, trapezoid, rhomboid). ▪ Base controls to achieve the desired degree of volume and/or indentation (overdirected, on base, underdirected, half-off base, off base). ▪ Choose the appropriate marcel iron diameter(s) to achieve desired results. ▪ Feed ends of the hair all the way through the marcel iron evenly to avoid crimped "fishhook" ends. ▪ Protect the scalp with a hard-rubber or nonflammable comb underneath the iron. ▪ Allow curls/hair to cool and set before applying finishing techniques. >> Perform finishing procedures as applicable: 1-2. **Relax** and **dry mold** the hair to reinforce the established lines of the design. 3. **Backbrush/backcomb** (optional) to create volume and indentation, expand the design's shape and/or connect shapes within the design. 4. **Define the form** to refine and achieve the desired finish. 5. **Detail** the hair to add your finishing touches and/or to personalize the design. >> Check for overall balance.
HAIR DESIGN COMPLETION	>> Reinforce client's satisfaction with overall salon experience. >> Make professional product recommendations. >> Prebook client's next appointment. >> End client's visit with warm and personal goodbye. >> Discard single-use supplies; disinfect tools and multi-use supplies; disinfect workstation and arrange in proper order. >> Complete client record. >> Wash hands.

PRESS AND CURL RUBRIC

Allotted Time: 1.5 Hours

Student Name: _____ ID Number: _____

Instructor: _____ Date: _____ Start Time: _____ End Time: _____

PRESS AND CURL (Live Model) – *Each scoring item is marked with either a "Yes" or "No." Each "Yes" counts for one point. Total number of points attainable is 35.*

CRITERIA	YES	NO	INSTRUCTOR ASSESSMENT
PREPARATION: *Did student...*			
1. Set up workstation with properly labeled supplies?	☐	☐	
2. Place disinfected tools and supplies at a visibly clean workstation?	☐	☐	
3. Wash their hands?	☐	☐	
Connect: Did student...			
4. Meet and greet client with a welcoming smile and pleasant tone?	☐	☐	
5. Communicate to build rapport and develop a relationship with client?	☐	☐	
6. Refer to client by name throughout service?	☐	☐	
Consult: Did student...			
7. Ask questions to discover client's wants and needs?	☐	☐	
8. Analyze client's hair and scalp and check for any contraindications?	☐	☐	
9. Gain feedback and consent from client before proceeding?	☐	☐	
PROCEDURE: *Did student...*			
10. Properly drape client and prepare for service?	☐	☐	
11. Ensure client protection and comfort by maintaining cape on outside of chair at all times?	☐	☐	
12. Carry out appropriate shampoo and condition procedures?	☐	☐	
13. Use products economically?	☐	☐	
Create: Did student...			
14. Apply thermal protectant product evenly through the hair?	☐	☐	
15. Air form the hair straight in the direction of the intended design?	☐	☐	
16. Test the temperature of the pressing comb and marcel iron prior to applying it to the hair?	☐	☐	
17. Apply the appropriate pressing technique according to the density and texture of hair?	☐	☐	
18. Press hair with the spine of the pressing comb?	☐	☐	
19. Press the entire hairline away from the face to achieve a smooth finish?	☐	☐	
20. Part and apply base controls to achieve volume and/or indentation with the marcel iron?	☐	☐	
21. Feed ends of the hair all the way through the marcel iron evenly to avoid crimped "fishhook" ends?	☐	☐	
22. Protect the scalp with a hard-rubber or nonflammable comb underneath the iron?	☐	☐	
23. Relax, define and detail the hair to achieve the desired finish?	☐	☐	
24. Check for balance in the final design?	☐	☐	
25. Teach client to use products to maintain the design at home?	☐	☐	
26. Practice infection control procedures and safety guidelines throughout service?	☐	☐	
COMPLETION (Complete): *Did student...*			
27. Ask questions and look for verbal and nonverbal cues to determine client's level of satisfaction?	☐	☐	
28. Make professional product recommendations?	☐	☐	
29. Ask client to make a future appointment?	☐	☐	
30. End client's visit with a warm and personal goodbye?	☐	☐	
31. Discard single-use supplies?	☐	☐	
32. Disinfect tools and multi-use supplies; disinfect workstation and arrange in proper order?	☐	☐	
33. Complete service within scheduled time?	☐	☐	
34. Complete client record?	☐	☐	
35. Wash their hands following service?	☐	☐	

COMMENTS: _____ TOTAL POINTS = _____ ÷ 35 = _____ %

Applying all aspects of a hair design service—from preparation to procedure to completion—each and every time you perform a hair design service will help you ensure client safety and satisfaction.

LESSONS LEARNED

Hair design client guidelines to follow to ensure comfort and satisfaction include:

Setting:

>> Distribute/Mold – Facing the client toward the mirror and discussing the direction of the design; monitoring the temperature of the blow dryer and explaining setting products used.

>> Scale – Avoiding pulling the hair and scratching the client with the tail comb.

>> Part/Apply – Ensuring the tip of the comb is smooth; protecting client's scalp from thermal irons; giving your client tips and hints on how to apply setting techniques at home; explaining how clients can adapt tool techniques at home.

Finishing:

>> Relax/Dry Mold – Using brushes that are easy on the scalp and don't cause discomfort; avoiding sharp or broken teeth and heavy pressure; ensuring your nails are not sharp or split to avoid scratching the scalp or pulling the hair.

>> Backbrushing/Backcombing – Avoiding excessive tension and pulling the hair; avoid matting the hair at the scalp; teaching the client how to remove backbrushed/backcombed hair from ends to base.

>> Define the Form – Controlling the amount of volume according to client's desires; checking for overall balance.

>> Detail – Adding finishing touches to personalize the design.

The three areas of a hair design service include the preparation, procedure and completion:

>> Preparation includes greeting the client, arranging workstation and performing a hair and scalp analysis.

>> Procedure includes the wet and thermal setting and finishing procedures used to ensure predictable results.

>> Completion includes reinforcing client's satisfaction, making product recommendations, rebooking next appointment and disinfecting workstation.

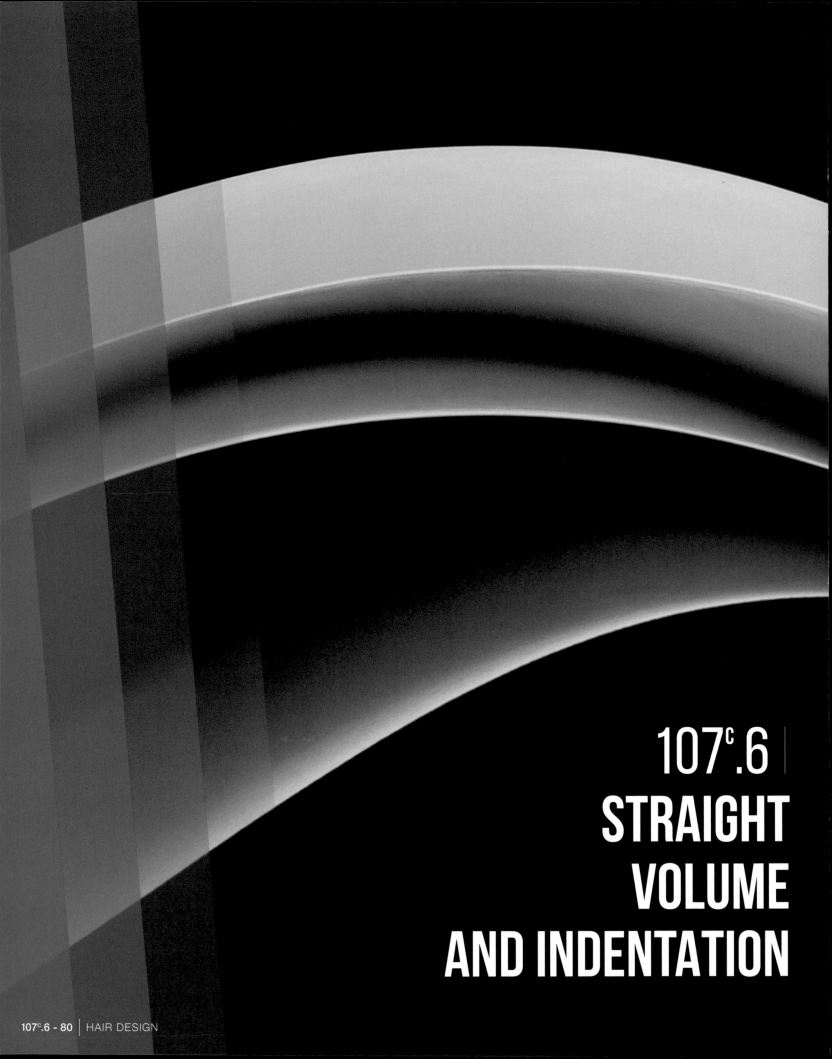

107ᶜ.6
STRAIGHT
VOLUME
AND INDENTATION

EXPLORE //

Can you identify three-dimensional forms that include depth, dimension and hollow spaces?

INSPIRE //

Using volume and indentation techniques will help you achieve voluminous wavy and flipped effects.

ACHIEVE //

Following this lesson on *Straight Volume and Indentation,* you'll be able to:

>> List the effects of the five straight volume tool positions

>> List the effects of the four straight indentation tool positions

>> Give examples of how rollers are set within straight shapes

>> Identify the base controls used in straight volume pincurls

FOCUS //

STRAIGHT VOLUME AND INDENTATION

Straight Base Control

Rollers in Straight Shapes

Pincurls in Straight Shapes

107^c.6 | STRAIGHT VOLUME AND INDENTATION

You have learned that hair design is arranging hair to create a temporary change in form, texture and direction. Now you will learn how to create straight volume, lift and fullness; as well as indentation and hollowness or depression. Straight indentation is usually combined with straight volume to create a contrast in direction. Straight volume and indentation is set within straight shapes to create directional movement.

STRAIGHT VOLUME

>> Creates lift and fullness

>> Base and strand are lifted and the ends turn under

STRAIGHT VOLUME AND INDENTATION

Straight indentation:

>> Creates areas of hollowness or depression

>> Base and strand are flat and the ends turn upward

Regardless of the technique or tool being used, straight volume and straight indentation base controls are performed within straight shapes, such as:

>> Rectangles

>> Triangles

>> Trapezoids

STRAIGHT BASE CONTROL

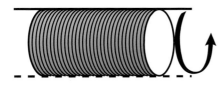

Base control refers to the size of the base in relation to the diameter of the tool, and the position of the tool in relation to the base. The base control used within a hair design affects the amount of volume (lift, fullness, mass) or closeness (flatness) achieved. Base control is used within straight and curvature shapes to create three-dimensional forms.

BASE SIZE

Base size includes both the width and the length of the base:

>> Base width is measured by diameter of the tool

>> Base length is measured by the length of the tool

The most commonly used base sizes are:

>> 1 diameter (1x)

>> 1½ diameters (1½x)

>> 2 diameters (2x)

In the case of pincurls, the size of the base is related to the diameter of the circle.

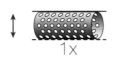

1x

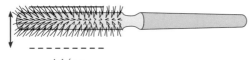

1½x

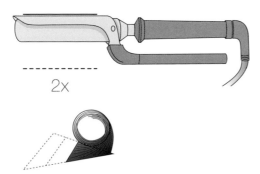

2x

1x

TOOL POSITION

The position of the tool in relation to the base will affect the lift or volume achieved as well as the amount of base strength. The base controls are the same regardless of the technique or tool being used (rollers, pincurls, round brush, thermal irons).

Straight Volume Tool Position

TOOL POSITION	BASE SIZE	PROJECTION ANGLE		DESCRIPTION	EFFECT	
On Base (Full Base)	1x		45° above the center of the base	Tool sits completely within the base		Maximum volume, maximum base strength
Half-Off Base (Half-Base)	1x Optional: 1½x, 2x		90° from the center of the base	Tool sits half-off and half-on the bottom parting		Less volume, less base strength
Off Base	1x Optional: 1½x, 2x		45° below the center of the base	Tool sits completely off the bottom parting		Least volume, least base strength
Underdirected	1½x Optional: 2x		90° from the center of the base	Tool sits in the lower portion of the base, but not on or below the parting		Reduced volume and base strength
Overdirected (Volume Base)	1½x Optional: 2x		45° above the center of the base	Tool sits in the upper portion of the base, but not on or above the parting		Exaggerated direction and volume, reduced base strength

Straight Indentation Tool Position

With indentation the position of the tool and the size of the base influence the amount of hollow space or flatness achieved. Tool position also influences the strength of the base and mobility of the curl.

TOOL POSITION	BASE SIZE	PROJECTION ANGLE	DESCRIPTION		EFFECT	
On Base	1x	60° below center		Tool sits completely within its base; rolled in an upward direction		Maximum base strength and volume
Half-Off Base	1x Optional: 1½x, 2x	30° below center		Tool sits half-off and half-on its base; rolled in an upward direction		Medium base strength, allowing more curl mobility
Off Base	1x Optional: 1½x, 2x	0° below center		Tool sits completely off its base; rolled in an upward direction		Minimum base strength, maximum curl mobility
Underdirected	1½x Optional: 2x	45° below center		Tool sits within the base close to the bottom of the parting; rolled in an upward direction		Medium base strength, strong curl flare

In summary, base size and tool position determine the amount of volume or indentation in a hair design.

COMPONENTS OF A CURL

There are three components of every curl:
>> Base
>> Stem (Arc)
>> Circle

TOOL

PINCURL

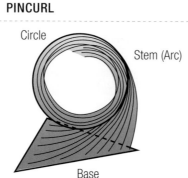

| Base | >> The area between straight and curved partings within a shape |
| | >> The section of hair on which the roller, thermal iron, round brush or pincurl is placed |

Stem (Arc)	>> The beginning portion of the hair between the scalp and the first turn of the hair around the roller, thermal iron, round brush or pincurl; the stem demonstrates the direction of the curl
	>> Determines the amount of movement of the section of hair
	■ Longer stems create more movement
	■ Shorter stems create more base strength (support) and less movement

Circle	>> The hair that is positioned around the tool such as the roller, thermal iron or round brush
	>> Determines the size of the curl
	>> Diameter of the tool you choose will determine the size of the circle
	>> The pincurl circle is the remaining end of the strand that forms the curl
	>> The size of the pincurl circle determines the width and strength of the wave
	■ A closed circle will produce a much smaller and stronger wave for a fluffy effect
	■ An open circle will produce a wider wave pattern with uniform curls

SALON**CONNECTION**

Make the Right Choice
In the salon, it's up to you to determine which tool and base controls to choose to achieve the effect the client desires. The key is to remember that the base controls are the same regardless of the tool chosen— rollers, round brushes or curling iron.

ROLLERS IN STRAIGHT SHAPES

>> Cylindrical rollers in various lengths and diameters are usually used within straight shapes.

>> Rollers set in straight shapes will achieve directional movement.

>> Hair is wrapped smoothly and evenly around the roller to avoid uneven texture and crimped ends.

>> Rollers chosen according to the desired curl patterns, repetition, alternation, progression or contrast.

>> Smaller rollers produce curlier effects.

>> Exact results will vary according to length of client's hair.

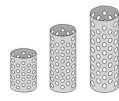

Rollers are used to set the hair and can achieve many of the same effects that pincurls do. So why choose rollers over pincurls?

>> One roller, depending on its length, sets the same amount of hair as two to four pincurls. This means that your setting time can be greatly reduced.

>> Setting with rollers allows you to set the hair with tension, which will result in a firmer, longer-lasting set.

ROLLERS WITHIN RECTANGLE SHAPES

A **rectangle** set with rollers will achieve straight directional movement.

>> Generally used as a "fill-in" or "blending" shape to set volume, with curvature shapes set on either side

>> Set from multiple points of origin

>> Base controls chosen according to desired effect

>> Straight indentation is generally positioned near the perimeter hairline for a "flip" effect

>> Horizontal partings are used to create base shapes

RECTANGLE

>> Rollers are all the same length

>> Roller diameter determines base width

>> Rollers can vary in diameter to achieve a progression of speeds

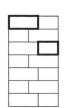

RECTANGLE – BRICKLAY PATTERN

>> Used when a larger area needs to be set

>> Various length rollers are used in a staggered alternating pattern of base divisions to avoid splits

ROLLERS WITHIN TRIANGLE SHAPES

Triangle shapes are used to achieve straight movement in any direction.

>> Progression of tool lengths is used to accommodate narrow to wide shape

>> Bricklay pattern can be used in wider area

>> Horizontal partings used to create base shapes

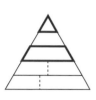

TRIANGLE

>> In this example, triangles radiate outward from one point of origin positioned at crown

>> Texture movement radiates outward from crown and gradually diminishes toward perimeter

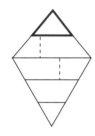

DIAMOND/KITE

>> Created by using back-to-back triangles

>> Achieves maximum texture at widest area of shape that gradually tapers toward narrow points of shape

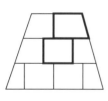

TRAPEZOID

>> Created with parallel distribution

>> Often used as a fill-in shape when curvature shapes are used on sides

>> Generally, a staggered or bricklay pattern is used to avoid splits

>> Can be thought of as a portion of the triangle

Setting Shapes With Thermal Tools

The same base controls used for rollers also apply to thermal tools.

The size of the base is determined by the diameter of the curling iron.

When air forming volume or indentation, the position, direction and continual motion of the brush controls the amount of volume and indentation achieved. For volume, the brush is positioned underneath the hairstrand. For indentation, the brush is positioned on top of the hairstrand.

DISCOVER**MORE**

Can You Imagine?

Can you imagine what you would do if you didn't have a blow dryer to style your hair? Believe it or not, your mom or grandmother probably had to set their hair in soda cans to get volume or a "bouffant" hairstyle. Some women used to sleep with soda cans in their hair, while others went to the salon to get the trendy look. Trends may come and go, but some techniques never die! Can you think of another way to create volume in the hair besides using rollers or cans? Search the Internet for some creative ideas, or come up with one of your own.

> Keeping bases consistent within a shape will allow you to work with equal amounts of hair in each pincurl and, therefore, have more consistent results in your finished curls/waves.

PINCURLS IN STRAIGHT SHAPES

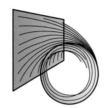

Generally, pincurls:

>> Are used on straight, permed or naturally curly hair that has been properly texturized

>> Are not recommended for tightly curled hair

>> Are used primarily to create temporary effects or specialized closeness

>> Allow a wide range of movement

Forming pincurls relies on your dexterity to create clean, smoothly wound curls without using tools. Smooth handling of the hair will control the consistency of the curl shape. If the pincurls are not smooth, the resulting curl or wave will not be smooth.

> Pincurls are one of many ways you are able to temporarily change the direction and texture of the hair.

BASE SHAPES FOR PINCURLS

Various shaped bases are used when working with pincurls. The primary reason for this is to avoid splits in the finished hair design. Generally, straight-shaped bases are used within straight shapes.

Straight pincurl base shapes most often used are:

>> Square/rectangle

>> Triangle

SQUARE/RECTANGLE

>> Usually used within a square or rectangle shape

TRIANGLE

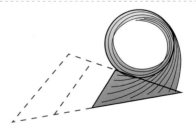

>> Used within straight shapes and along the hairline

>> Alternating triangles help avoid splits

BASE CONTROL FOR PINCURLS

Pincurl base control refers to:

>> The size of the base in relation to the size of the circle or curl

>> The position of the curl relative to the base

The size of the base and the base control used will affect the length of the stem of each pincurl. The length of the stem will determine the movement of the curl.

The size of a pincurl base is usually related to the diameter of the circle, which determines the resulting wave/curl.

Straight volume pincurl base controls most often used are:

>> On base
>> Half-off base
>> Off base

PINCURL POSITION/BASE SIZE		DESCRIPTION	EFFECT
On-Base Pincurl (No-Stem Pincurl) 1x		Entire circle of the curl is positioned on the base.	>> Produces lift or strong curl effect >> When used in a series, creates a wave line
Half-Off Base Pincurl (Half-Stem Pincurl) 1x Optional: 1½x, 2x		Half of the circle is positioned below the base.	>> Equal degree of predetermined direction or volume
Off-Base Pincurl (Full-Stem Pincurl) 1x Optional: 1½x, 2x		Stem and circle are positioned below the base.	>> Design closeness and mobility, usually in the nape area or along the hairline

The same base controls apply to indentation pincurls.

Forming Straight Volume Pincurls

Straight volume pincurls are large, stand-up pincurls that achieve a similar effect to hair wound around a roller, but result in weaker (less) volume.

>> **Used within straight shapes to create fullness and height**

>> **Referred to as stand-up, cascade pincurls and barrel curls**

In some instances, you will need to create a blend or transition from areas of volume to areas of closeness. Transitional or semi-stand-up pincurls will achieve this blend. These pincurls are not quite stand-up curls and not quite flat curls.

REINFORCE ARC

>> Distribute hair smoothly

>> Use tail of comb to reinforce arc

SMOOTH (RIBBON)

>> Smooth hairstrand to create a ribbon-like effect

>> Smooth ends in direction of circle formation

FORM CIRCLE

>> Place ends inside to form circle

SECURE

>> Secure through the circle to the base with clip

Base size and tool position determine the amount of volume or indentation in a hair design. The tools you work with will be determined by the desired results, your client's hair and your personal preferences.

LESSONS LEARNED

The effects of the five straight volume tool positions are:

>> On Base – Maximum volume, maximum base strength

>> Half-Off Base – Less volume, less base strength

>> Off Base – Least volume, least base strength

>> Underdirected – Reduced volume and base strength

>> Overdirected – Exaggerated direction and volume, reduced base strength

The effects of the four straight indentation tool positions are:

>> On Base – Maximum base strength and volume

>> Half-Off Base – Medium base strength, allowing more curl mobility

>> Off Base – Minimum base strength, maximum curl mobility

>> Underdirected – Medium base strength, strong curl flare

The three components of a curl are:
>> Base
>> Stem (Arc)
>> Circle

Rollers can be set in straight shapes such as rectangles, triangles and trapezoids by using:

>> The same length and size of rollers

>> A progression of roller diameters and/or lengths

>> A bricklay pattern

The base controls used for straight volume pincurls are on base, half-off base and off base.

BRICKLAY ROLLERS

EXPLORE

What common pattern do you see within a brick wall?

INSPIRE

The bricklay setting pattern creates a strong foundation with versatile styling options.

ACHIEVE

Following the *Bricklay – Rollers Workshop*, you'll be able to:

>> Create a design with straight volume that moves away from the face and sides

>> Set a bricklay pattern with rollers and pincurls using the one-two method

Curvature movement moves away from the face and blends to activated texture.

Straight volume is set within a bricklay pattern using the one-two method. A progression of roller diameters and pincurls are used to accommodate the lengths.

WET-SETTING PROCEDURES – RECTANGLE/BRICKLAY

1. DISTRIBUTE: Parallel

2. MOLD:
   Curved parallel distribution

3. SCALE: N/A

4. PART:
   Rectangular bases | Triangular bases

5. APPLY:
   One-two method | Straight volume rollers and pincurls
   1x on
   1x half-off

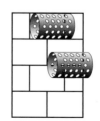
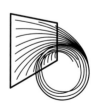

DESIGN DECISIONS CHART

BRICKLAY – ROLLERS

Draw or fill in the boxes with the appropriate answers.

DESIGN DECISIONS

STRUCTURE	FORM/TEXTURE		
DISTRIBUTE			
MOLD/SCALE			
PART/APPLY			
FINISH/DIRECTION			

Instructor Signature _____ **Date** _____

BRICKLAY – ROLLERS

View the video, complete the Design Decisions chart, then perform
this workshop. Complete the self-check as you progress through
the workshop.

40 mins
Suggested
Salon Speed

PREPARATION	✔
>> Assemble tools and products >> Set up workstation	☐

DISTRIBUTE AND MOLD

1. **Distribute and mold hair away from face using straight and curved parallel distribution:** >> Apply setting product to hair >> Mold hair away from face downward toward nape >> Mold hair on sides in a curved movement using curved parallel distribution	☐

TOP AND SIDES

2. **Bases are staggered from front hairline to nape using one-two method.**	
3. **Part and apply first row using 1x on-base control:** >> Begin at center front hairline >> Measure base size using length and width of roller >> Project 45° above center >> Position and secure roller within rectangular shaped base parallel to bottom parting >> Use shorter length rollers to accommodate hairline	☐
4. **Part and apply second row to begin one-two method:** >> Create a center part behind first roller >> Measure base size using length and width of roller >> Project 45° above center >> Position and secure roller 1x on base >> Repeat base control on opposite side of center part to establish one-two method	☐

5. **Complete second row as you work toward hairline on both sides:**
   >> Use slight diagonal-forward partings
   >> 1x on base

TRANSITION ZONE/CROWN AREA

6. **Continue one-two method:**
   >> Position a 1x on-base roller in center of next row
   >> Part triangular bases on either side of center roller
   >> 1x on base

7. **Part and apply next row 1x on base working from center toward either side of hairline.**

   Note: The triangular bases at the crown area do not extend to the hairline. This will allow you to transition over the curve of the head.

8. **Part and apply lower crown with half-off base control to reduce volume:**
   >> Project 90° from center of base
   >> Adjust angle of parting to adapt to curves of head
   >> Position and secure roller 1x half-off base
   >> Work from center to either side

BACK

9. **Continue to set back with 1x half-off base control:**
   >> Adapt length and diameter of roller as hair becomes shorter

10. Part and apply perimeter in volume pincurls:

>> 1x half-off or off-base control
>> Stagger bases to avoid splits

DRY HAIR

11. Dry hair thoroughly under dryer:

>> Once dry, allow hair to cool, then remove all tools
>> Drying time will vary according to hair length and density, and is not included in suggested salon speed

FINISH — COMB-OUT

12. Relax set with cushion brush(es):

>> Begin at nape
>> Brush lengths thoroughly to blend bases

13. Dry mold hair in direction of set:

>> Reinforce lines of design using a cushion brush

14. Backbrush in direction of design using one-stroke technique:

>> Hold parting of hair firmly between fingers
>> Slide brush down surface of hair toward base; turn wrist to lock backbrushed hair to base, then release brush carefully
>> Use bristles of brush to pick up next section
>> Connect bases using same backbrushing technique
>> Work from center to back, and to either side as you blend bases

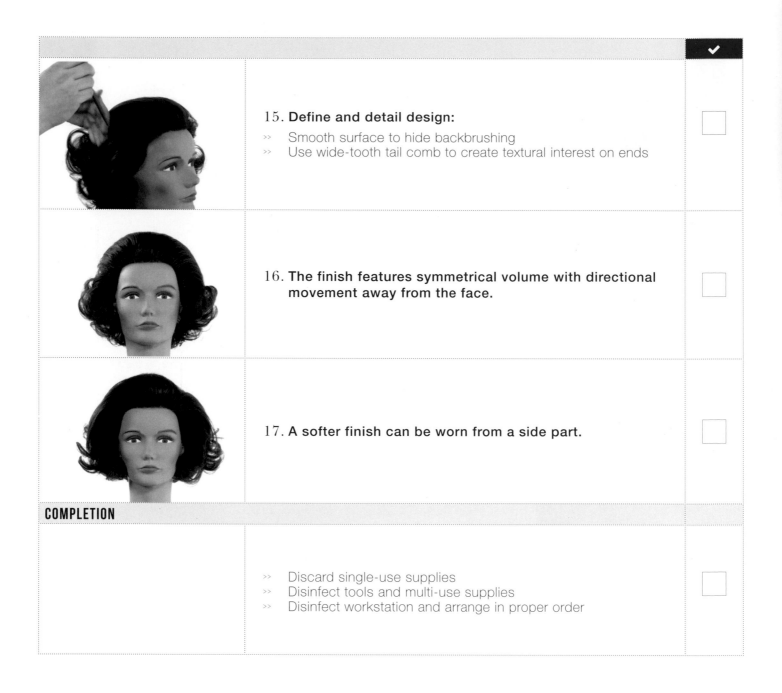

15. **Define and detail design:**
    » Smooth surface to hide backbrushing
    » Use wide-tooth tail comb to create textural interest on ends

16. **The finish features symmetrical volume with directional movement away from the face.**

17. **A softer finish can be worn from a side part.**

COMPLETION

» Discard single-use supplies
» Disinfect tools and multi-use supplies
» Disinfect workstation and arrange in proper order

40 mins
Suggested Salon Speed

My Speed
_____
_____
_____

INSTRUCTIONS:
Record your time in comparison with the suggested salon speed. Then, list here how you could improve your performance.

_____
_____
_____
_____
_____

CURVATURE VOLUME AND INDENTATION | 107ᶜ.8

EXPLORE //

Can you identify natural or manmade objects that consist of curved lines?

INSPIRE //

Graceful, calming, dynamic
and unpredictable—curved
lines express fluidity.

ACHIEVE //

Following this lesson on
*Curvature Volume and
Indentatio*n, you'll be able to:

>> Identify curvature volume
and curvature indentation
base controls

>> Identify base shapes
used to set various
curvature shapes

>> Describe the position
of rollers within various
curvature shapes

>> Explain the effects
of the three types of
curvature pincurls

FOCUS //

**CURVATURE VOLUME
AND INDENTATION**

Curvature Base Control

Rollers in Curvature Shapes

Pincurls in Curvature Shapes

107ᶜ.8 | CURVATURE VOLUME AND INDENTATION

Curvature volume and indentation setting techniques are used to create three-dimensional forms with contrasting direction and texture. Curvature volume is mass or fullness and is applied within curvature shapes. Curvature indentation causes the hair to flare out and is generally used with curvature volume.

CURVATURE VOLUME

>> Creates lift

>> Base and strand are lifted, and the ends turn under

CURVATURE INDENTATION

>> Creates areas of hollowness and depression

>> Strand is flat, and the ends turn upward

Regardless of the technique or tool being used, curvature volume and indentation are set within curvature shapes in either a clockwise or counterclockwise direction. The three common shapes used to set curvature volume and indentation are the circle, oval and oblong.

>> **CIRCLE**	>> **OVAL**	>> **OBLONG**

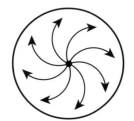 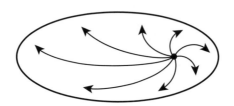 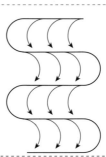

CURVATURE BASE CONTROL

Base control refers to the size of the base in relation to the diameter of the tool, and the position of the tool in relation to the base. The base control used within a hair design affects the amount of volume (lift, fullness, mass) or closeness (flatness) achieved. The base controls that are used in hair designing are the same, regardless of the technique or tool being used (rollers, round brush, thermal irons or pincurls). The base shapes used for curvature volume and indentation are:

>> Triangle   >> Trapezoid   >> Rhomboid

BASE SIZE AND TOOL POSITION

>> Base size includes both the width and the length of the base

>> Base width is measured by the diameter of the tool

>> Base length is measured by the length of the tool

>> Base sizes include 1x, 1½x and 2x

>> When using rollers, the large end of the roller is used to measure the base size

>> Curvature volume tool positions:
- On base
- Underdirected
- Half-off base
- Off base

>> There are no overdirected tool positions in curvature volume

1x On Base
45° Above Center
Maximum Volume

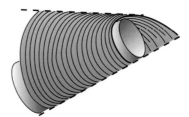

1½x Underdirected
90° From Center
Medium Volume

Curvature Volume Tool Position

BASE CONTROL	BASE SIZE
On Base	1x
Underdirected	1½x, 2x
Half-Off Base	1x, 1½x, 2x
Off Base	1x, 1½x, 2x

1x Half-Off Base
90° From Center
Minimum Volume

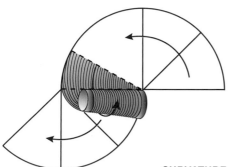

1x Off Base
45° Below Center
Least Volume

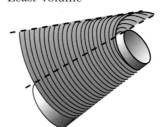

Curvature Indentation Tool Position

Although the position of the tool changes when setting curvature indentation, the base controls are the same. The roller is positioned on top of the hairstrand, and the roller is rolled upward toward the base.

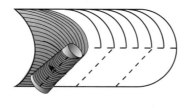

CURVATURE INDENTATION

In summary, curvature volume and indentation are used within curvature shapes, such as the circle, oval and oblong to create mass, fullness and flare within a design. The base controls chosen will determine the final effect, ranging from maximum to least volume.

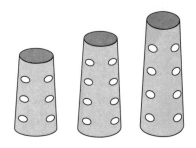

ROLLERS IN CURVATURE SHAPES

The most efficient way to set rollers within a curvature shape, such as the circle, oval or oblong, is to use cone-shaped, or tapered, rollers. Cone-shaped rollers consist of a progression of speeds. They also consist of a small end and a large end. Because of the way cone-shaped rollers fit into a curvature shape, they allow you to create stronger curvature movements that are not achievable with cylindrical rollers.

ROLLERS WITHIN A HALF-CIRCLE

HALF-CIRCLE:

>> Curvature volume throughout the shape moves and directs the hair equally away and then toward the face

>> Consists of equal radial lines

>> Generally positioned at the fringe area or at the sides

>> Equal-length rollers are positioned one diameter away from a single center point of origin

SALON**CONNECTION**

Compose Unique Hair Designs

In the salon, it's up to you to consult with your client in order to determine the appropriate shapes, tools and techniques to use in order to fulfill the client's vision. The key is to apply your knowledge of curvature volume and indentation theory along with straight volume and indentation theory to compose unique hair designs—all the while remembering that the same base controls and techniques apply to all shapes, regardless of the tool chosen.

DISTRIBUTE

>> One point of origin

>> Radial distribution

MOLD

>> Curved lines

>> Do not disturb point of origin

>> In this example, the hair is molded in a counterclockwise direction

SCALE

>> Small diameter plus length of roller away from point of origin

PART

>> Base area is measured with the large end of a cone-shaped roller at the circumference of the shape

>> Parting is taken from single point of origin to outside of shape to create a triangle-shaped base

>> Note that the base length is established when scaling the shape, small end of the roller plus length

APPLY

>> Roller is angled toward point of origin

>> Roller is rolled toward back of shape

>> Roller is positioned one diameter away from point of origin

>> Roller is positioned parallel to the bottom parting

Secure

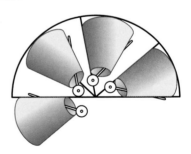

>> Each roller is secured at the small end with its forces

>> In this example, a progression of base controls from on base to off base achieves maximum to diminishing volume

>> Rollers can be secured with a pick or a double-prong clip

ROLLERS WITHIN AN EXPANDED CIRCLE

EXPANDED CIRCLE:

>> Extension of a half-circle that encompasses a larger area than a half-circle

>> Consists of equal radial lines

>> Most often positioned at the fringe area and/or sides to create curved movement that extends to the back

>> Same distribution and molding rules apply as with the half-circle, with the exception that a larger area is scaled according to the size desired

>> Set using an inner-and-outer technique

DISCOVER**MORE**

Nature's Clever Three-Dimensional Forms

What do the lotus, morning glory, passion and snowdrop flowers all have in common? They all have the ability to open and close their petals—revealing distinctly different forms. When closed, these flowers collapse and can resemble circular, oval, oblong and triangular shapes, and as they open, their "true" form begins to expand as they reveal and display their individual petals, stamens and pistils. Some petals radiate outward from a central point of origin, while others consist of parallel vein-like tendrils. Nature is abundant with three-dimensional curvilinear forms that include radial and parallel lines that you can use as inspiration when creating hair designs. Search the Internet for time-lapse videos, of an iris for example, to see how these extraordinary flowers expand and close their forms.

DISTRIBUTE

>> One point of origin

>> Radial distribution

MOLD

>> Curved lines

>> Do not disturb point of origin

>> In this example, the hair is molded in a counterclockwise direction

SCALE

>> Measure shape with rollers to be used (cone for inner; cone and/or cylinder for outer shape)

>> Inner circle – Measure small diameter plus length of roller away from point of origin

>> Outer circle – Measure with the length of the roller

PART AND APPLY

Inner Circle:
>> Set using the same techniques as a normal half-circle

Outer Circle:
>> Align base partings from same point of origin as inner circle

>> Measure with the large end of a cone-shaped roller at the outer circumference of the shape

>> Set outer circle by matching the large end of the cone-shaped roller from the inner circle:
- For a progression of speed, use a cone-shaped roller
- For a consistent rate of speed, use a cylinder roller

Secure

>> Secure at the small end of the roller

ROLLERS WITHIN A HALF-OVAL

HALF-OVAL:

» Positioned at the front or sides, half-ovals direct a greater amount of hair off the face than on the face, or the reverse, a smaller amount of hair off the face and a greater amount on the face

» Consists of unequal radial lines

» Generally, only a portion of the oval is used

» Consists of an off-center point of origin

» Set with unequal-length rollers
   ▪ Shorter rollers/Fast speed
   ▪ Longer rollers/Slow speed

» Rollers are positioned one diameter (small end) away from point of origin

» Greater amount of hair on the face

» Shorter to longer rollers

» Smaller amount of hair on the face

» Longer to shorter rollers

ROLLERS WITHIN AN EXPANDED OVAL

EXPANDED OVAL:

>> An extension of the half-oval used to encompass a larger area than the half-oval

>> Consists of unequal radial lines

>> Positioned at the top-front or sides of the head to create curvature movement that travels toward the back

>> Set using the indirect technique

DISTRIBUTE/MOLD/SCALE

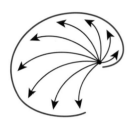 

>> Off-center point of origin

>> Same distribution and molding rules apply as with the half-oval

>> Scale according to the area to be encompassed

PART/APPLY

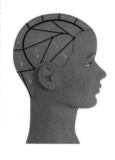  

>> Partings are created using the indirect technique

>> Base size is measured with the large end of the cone-shaped roller

>> First roller is set using the original point of origin

>> Each subsequent roller is set from its own point of origin that is established at the front bottom corner of each previous roller

>> Rollers are positioned one diameter (small end) away from their point of origin

>> To close the shape, partings are taken from the original point of origin

>> Secured at the small end of the roller

ROLLERS WITHIN AN OBLONG

OBLONGS:

>> Generally, two or more oblongs are set in alternating (opposite) directions to create a strong wave pattern

>> Oblongs may be positioned anywhere on the head and in any direction

>> Rollers are positioned diagonally within rhomboid-shaped bases from many points of origin

>> When volume is combined with indentation, a "flipped" effect is achieved

DISTRIBUTE

>> 1st direction toward convex end

>> 2nd direction toward concave end

MOLD

>> Parallel curved lines

>> Position finger firmly in middle of oblong when molding the 2nd direction to avoid disturbing the 1st direction

SCALE

>> Place roller diagonally

>> Scale shape from convex to concave end

PART

>> Begin at convex end

>> Measure base size with large end of roller

>> Part 45° in 1st direction to create a rhomboid-shaped base

APPLY

>> Position small end of roller in the 1st direction

>> Position roller under the hairstrand and roll toward the base

Secure

>> Secure at the small end of the roller

>> Same distribution and molding rules apply as with the volume oblong, with the exception of scaling

>> Scale by positioning the roller vertically, or 1½x the length of the tool, to create a larger shape

>> Begin setting at the concave end

>> Part in the 2nd direction from the center of the oblong

>> Position roller on top of the hairstrand

>> Roll upward and position roller in the 2nd direction

>> Do not disturb 1st direction, which creates the hollow space

>> Secure at the small end of the roller

SETTING SHAPES WHEN AIR FORMING
WITH A ROUND BRUSH

>> The same distribution, molding and scaling rules that apply to rollers also apply to air forming with a round brush

>> The same base controls used for rollers also apply to a round brush

>> The size of the base is determined by the diameter of the round brush

>> When air forming volume or indentation, it is the position, direction and continual motion of the round brush that controls the amount of volume and indentation achieved

>> For indentation, the brush is positioned on top of the hairstrand

>> For volume, the brush is positioned underneath the hairstrand

PINCURLS IN CURVATURE SHAPES

Generally, curvature pincurls allow for a wide range of movement. Consulting with your client and visualizing the finished design will help you determine where lift (volume) and where a closer effect is desired. Curvature pincurls are used on straight, permed or naturally curly hair that has been properly texturized and are not recommended for tightly curled hair.

Curved or crescent-shaped partings are used for setting curvature pincurls. The size of the base and position of the circle in relation to the base affect the amount of volume and indentation achieved.

Curvature volume and indentation pincurls are set within curvature shapes, such as the:

>> Half-circle   >> Half-oval   >> Oblong

When setting curvature volume pincurls within a half-circle, all pincurls are positioned at an equal distance away from the point of origin.

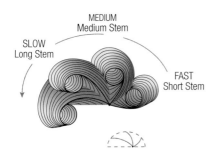

When setting curvature volume pincurls within a half-oval, the pincurls are positioned at an unequal distance away from the point of origin to achieve fast, medium and slow speeds.

Base controls for curvature pincurls are:

>> On base   >> Half-off base   >> Off base

ON BASE (NO STEM)	**HALF-OFF BASE** (HALF-STEM)	**OFF BASE** (FULL STEM)
	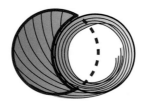	

CURVATURE PINCURLS

The three common types of curvature pincurls are:
>> **Flat**   >> **Volume**   >> **Indentation**

In the following example, flat, volume and indentation pincurls are set within alternating oblongs (shapings) to achieve a wave pattern with flare. Flat, volume and indentation pincurls are set from multiple points of origin.

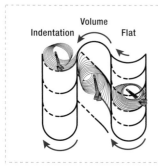

Keep the following key points in mind when creating **flat** pincurls.

Flat pincurls are used for closeness
>> The hair does not travel any distance from the base before the stem (arc) begins; the result is a no-stem curl

>> Base, stem (arc) and circle are flat

>> Also known as carved or sculpture curls

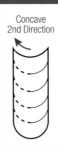

Concave
2nd Direction

>> Flat pincurls begin at the concave, or open, end of the shape

>> In this example, a clockwise oblong is distributed, molded and scaled vertically

>> A tail comb is used to part the hair from the center of the shape in the 2nd direction, toward the concave end

>> The hairstrand is then smoothed with the teeth of the comb and thumb to create a ribbon-like effect

>> The base remains flat while the stem is curved, and the circle is formed

>> The circle is positioned in front of its base

>> The flat pincurl is secured in the 2nd direction with a clip

>> This technique is repeated until the remaining shape is completed

>> **Volume pincurls are used to create fullness and height** and can be positioned anywhere on the head

>> Base and stem (arc) are lifted away from the head, and the circle turns under

Convex
1st Direction

>> Volume pincurls begin at the convex, or closed, end of the shape

>> In this example, a counterclockwise oblong is molded and scaled vertically

>> A tail comb is used to part the hair in the 1st direction, toward the convex end

>> The tail comb is used to create lift at the base and to reinforce the stem (arc)

>> The hairstrand is then smoothed to create a ribbon-like effect

>> The circle is formed

>> The volume pincurl is secured through the circle in the 1st direction

>> This technique is repeated until the remaining shape is completed

Keep the following key points in mind when creating **indentation** pincurls.

>> **Indentation pincurls are used to create hollow space and flare**

>> Base is flat and the stem (arc) and circle are lifted

>> Generally, indentation pincurls follow volume pincurls in a hair design

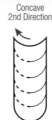
Concave
2nd Direction

>> Indentation pincurls begin at the concave, open end of the shape

>> In this example, a clockwise oblong is molded and scaled vertically

>> A tail comb is used to part the hair from the center of the shape in the 2nd direction

>> The index finger is used to keep the base flat while curving the stem (arc) with the comb

>> The hairstrand is then smoothed to create a ribbon-like effect

>> The circle is formed up and away from the base

>> The circle is positioned in the upper portion of its base and secured through the circle in the 2nd direction

>> This technique is repeated until the entire shape is completed

LESSONS LEARNED

Curvature volume and curvature indentation base controls include on base, underdirected, half-off base and off base. Common base sizes are 1x, 1½x and 2x. These base controls are used with any tool when setting curvature shapes.

Triangle-shaped bases are used to set a half-circle and half-oval, while trapezoid-shaped bases are used to set the expanded circle. Rhomboid-shaped bases are used to set oblongs.

The position of rollers within various curvature shapes can be described as:
>> Half-circle – Equal length rollers are positioned 1x away from a center point of origin

>> Expanded circle – Rollers are positioned 1x away from point of origin in the inner circle; roller encompasses length of base in the outer circle

>> Half-oval – Unequal length rollers are positioned 1x away from an off-center point of origin

>> Expanded oval – Rollers are positioned 1x away from the front bottom corner of the previous roller

>> Oblongs – For volume, rollers are positioned diagonally with the small end in the 1st direction encompassing the length of base; for indentation, rollers are positioned diagonally with the small end in the 2nd direction with the 1st direction left undisturbed

The effects of the three types of curvature pincurls are:
>> Flat to achieve closeness

>> Volume to achieve fullness and height

>> Indentation to create hollow space and flare

HALF-CIRCLE/RECTANGLE
ROLLERS AND PINCURLS

EXPLORE

Can you name natural or manmade objects that consist of a circular shape?

INSPIRE

Learning to set hair in partial circles allows you to create curvature movements within a hair design.

ACHIEVE

Following this *Half-Circle/Rectangle – Rollers and Pincurls Workshop*, you'll be able to:

>> Create a design with curvature and straight volume that moves half away from the face and half toward the face

>> Set and comb out a half-circle with rollers

>> Set and comb out an expanded circle with rollers and pincurls using the inner/outer technique

>> Set and comb out a rectangle with rollers and pincurls

Curvature volume, half away from the face and half toward the face, blends to activated texture.

Rollers set in the half-circle create movement half away and half toward the face.

Expanded circles at the sides are set with a progression of roller diameters and volume pincurls. The bricklay pattern in the back is set with rollers and pincurls.

WET-SETTING PROCEDURES – HALF-CIRCLE, EXPANDED CIRCLE

	HALF-CIRCLE	EXPANDED CIRCLE
1. DISTRIBUTE: Radial	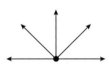	
2. MOLD: Curved radial Curved parallel		
3. SCALE: Half-circle Expanded circle		
4. PART: Triangular bases Trapezoid-shaped bases		
5. APPLY: Half-circle, cone-shaped rollers Inner/outer technique, cone-shaped rollers and volume pincurls	›› 1x on base ›› 1¹/2x underdirected ›› 1x half-off base ›› 1x off base	›› 1x half-off base

DESIGN DECISIONS CHART

HALF-CIRCLE/RECTANGLE – ROLLERS AND PINCURLS

Draw or fill in the boxes with the appropriate answers.

DESIGN DECISIONS

SHAPE/WEIGHT

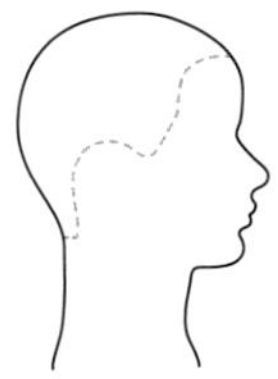

FORM/TEXTURE

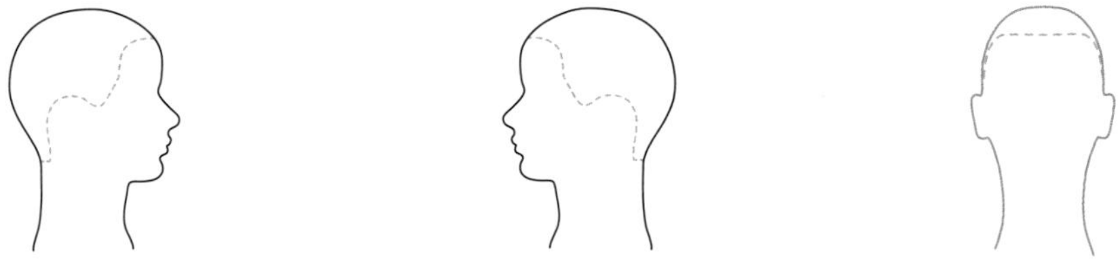

DISTRIBUTE

MOLD/SCALE

PART/APPLY

FINISH/DIRECTION

Instructor Signature ______________________________ **Date** ______________

PERFORMANCE GUIDE

HALF-CIRCLE/RECTANGLE
ROLLERS AND PINCURLS

View the video, complete the Design Decisions chart, then perform this workshop. Complete the self-check as you progress through the workshop.

40 mins
Suggested
Salon Speed

PREPARATION	✔
>> Assemble tools and products >> Set up workstation	☐

DISTRIBUTE/MOLD/SCALE

1. Distribute/mold/scale half-circle at front hairline:

>> Apply styling gel evenly through clean, wet hair
>> Distribute hair from center point of origin using radial distribution
>> Mold hair in counterclockwise direction
>> Scale out half-circle using small diameter plus length of roller
>> Secure ends in a flat, circular shape

☐

2. Distribute/mold/scale an expanded circle on right side:

>> Distribute hair from center point of origin using radial distribution
>> Mold hair in counterclockwise direction
>> Measure expanded circle according to size of desired area
>> Scale inner circle using small diameter plus length of roller
>> Scale outer circle using length of roller
>> Secure ends in a circular shape

☐

3. Distribute/mold/scale a clockwise expanded circle on left side.

☐

4. Distribute and mold remaining hair:

>> Distribute hair using parallel distribution
>> Mold hair straight down
>> Secure ends

☐

5. **The half-circle is set with cone-shaped rollers:**
   - » 1x on base
   - » 1½x underdirected
   - » 1x half-off base
   - » 1x off-base control
   - » Base size is measured with large end of cone-shaped roller
   - » Roller is positioned one diameter (small end) away from point of origin
   - » Roller is positioned parallel to the bottom parting
   - » Roller is secured at small end

6. **Part and apply first roller:**
   - » 1x on base

7. **Part and apply second roller:**
   - » 1½x underdirected base control

8. **Part and apply third roller:**
   - » 1x half-off base control

9. **Part and apply fourth roller:**
   - » 1x off-base control

PART AND APPLY – EXPANDED CIRCLE

10. **Expanded circles are set on sides using inner/outer technique:**
    - » Inner circle is set with triangular bases
      - ■ Rollers are positioned one diameter (small end) away from point of origin
    - » Outer circle is set with trapezoid-shaped bases
      - ■ Base sizes are equal to length of conical-shaped roller
    - » All rollers are positioned parallel to bottom parting
    - » Last 2 partings in outer circle are set with volume pincurls

11. **Part and apply inner circle using cone-shaped rollers:**
   >> Part from center point of origin
   >> 1x half-off base control
   >> Position roller away from point of origin, parallel to base parting
   >> Secure at small end

12. **Outer circle is set with cone-shaped rollers and volume pincurls:**
   >> Trapezoid-shaped bases are measured with large end of roller
   >> Parting extends from center point of origin

13. **Part and apply outer circle**
   >> 1x half-off base control
   >> Position rollers parallel to bottom parting and secure at small end of roller
   >> Set last partings with volume pincurls

14. **Part and apply inner/outer circle on opposite side.**

PART AND APPLY – BRICKLAY PATTERN

15. **Bricklay pattern is set from maximum to diminished volume within rectangular bases:**
   >> Cylindrical rollers:
      ■ 1x on base
      ■ 1x on base
      ■ 1x half-off base
   >> Volume pincurls:
      ■ 1x half-off base
      ■ 1x half-off base

16. **Part and apply first roller 1x on base.**

☐

17. **Continue to part and apply volume base control within a bricklay pattern:**
   >> 1x on base
   >> 1x half-off base
   >> Adapt roller lengths to fit area
   >> Stagger base partings to avoid splits

☐

18. **Part and apply remaining lengths with volume pincurls:**
   >> Diameter of pincurl circle should correspond to small-diameter roller
   >> 1x half-off base
   >> Stagger bases to avoid splits
   >> Secure with clips

☐

DRY HAIR

19. **Dry hair thoroughly under dryer:**
   >> Once dried, allow hair to cool; then remove all tools

   Note: Drying time will vary according to hair length and density, and is not included in suggested salon speed.

☐

FINISH — COMB-OUT ✔

20. Relax set with cushion brush(es) to thoroughly blend bases:

» Work from nape to sides and then to top

21. Dry-mold by retracing directions of design:

» Begin in the half-circle, blend into expanded circles on sides and then into back

22. Backbrush hair in direction of set to create volume and support:

» Begin in the half-circle using one-stroke technique

23. Continue backbrushing into expanded circle, then into back and nape.

24. Define and detail design:

» Smooth surface to hide backbrushing
» Use wide-tooth tail comb to add surface texture and definition

25. The finish shows curvature volume that moves half-off and half toward the face, blending to straight volume in back, with perimeter texture.

COMPLETION

>> Discard single-use supplies
>> Disinfect tools and multi-use supplies
>> Disinfect workstation and arrange in proper order

40 mins
Suggested
Salon Speed

My Speed

_____
_____
_____

INSTRUCTIONS

Record your time in comparison with the suggested salon speed. Then, list here how you could improve your performance.

_____

_____

_____

_____

_____

EXPANDED OVALS
ROLLERS

EXPLORE

How did the oval get its name?

INSPIRE

Expanded ovals in a hair design are easily created using the indirect technique.

ACHIEVE

Following this *Expanded Ovals – Rollers Workshop*, you'll be able to:

>> Create a design with curvature and straight volume that moves predominately away from the face

>> Set and comb-out an expanded oval with rollers using the indirect technique

>> Set and comb-out a rectangle with rollers

Straight volume at the top plus curvature volume at the sides moves the hair away from the face and results in a progression of curl textures.

Expanded ovals are set with rollers at the sides using the indirect technique.

A rectangle shape is set at the top moving away from the face. A bricklay pattern is set in the back with a progression of roller diameters and base controls.

WET-SETTING PROCEDURES – EXPANDED OVALS

1. DISTRIBUTE: Radial

2. MOLD: Curved radial

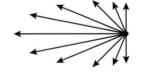

3. SCALE: Expanded oval

4. PART:
   Triangular bases | Multiple points of origin

5. APPLY:
   Indirect technique | Cone-shaped rollers | 1x half off

DESIGN DECISIONS CHART

EXPANDED OVALS – ROLLERS

Draw or fill in the boxes with the appropriate answers.

DESIGN DECISIONS			
STRUCTURE	FORM/TEXTURE		
DISTRIBUTE			
MOLD/SCALE			
PART/APPLY			
FINISH/DIRECTION			

Instructor Signature _____ **Date** _____

EXPANDED OVALS – ROLLERS

View the video, complete the Design Decisions chart, then perform this workshop. Complete the self-check as you progress through the workshop.

30 mins
Suggested
Salon Speed

PREPARATION		✔
	>> Assemble tools and products >> Set up workstation	☐

DISTRIBUTE, MOLD AND SCALE		
	1. Distribute, mold and scale a rectangle shape on top: >> Parallel distribution from front hairline toward crown >> Scale out rectangle using length of roller >> Secure ends with clip	☐
	2. Distribute, mold and scale an oval shape on right side: >> Radial distribution >> Mold counterclockwise >> Scale shape using a tail comb >> Secure ends with clip	☐
	3. Distribute, mold and scale an oval shape on left side: >> Radial distribution >> Mold clockwise >> Scale shape using tail comb >> Secure ends with clip	☐

	✓

4. **Distribute remaining back lengths straight downward and secure.**

PART AND APPLY – TOP – RECTANGLE

5. **Part and apply first roller 1x half-off base control:**
   >> Begin at front hairline
   >> Distribute hair at 90° projection angle from center of base
   >> Secure roller parallel to bottom parting

6. **Set remaining rectangle shape 1x half-off base.**

PART AND APPLY – SIDES – EXPANDED OVAL

7. **Expanded ovals on sides are set using indirect technique with cone-shaped rollers:**
   >> After first roller is set, each new point of origin is located at front-bottom corner of previous roller

8. **Part and apply first roller 1x half-off base:**
   >> Part from point of origin to perimeter of shape
   >> Position small end of roller one diameter away from point of origin
   >> Secure at small end of roller

9. **Part and apply next roller using indirect technique:**
   >> Part from front bottom corner of previous roller to perimeter of shape
   >> 1x half-off base control
   >> Position and secure roller parallel to bottom parting

10. **Repeat same setting procedures to complete outer perimeter of shape:**
    >> Use front bottom corner of previous roller as point of origin

    Note: A larger diameter roller is used in the perimeter to correspond to longer lengths.

11. **Part and apply remainder of shape using original point of origin:**
    >> 1x half-off base control

12. **Part and apply opposite side using same procedures and indirect technique.**

PART AND APPLY – BACK – BRICKLAY PATTERN

13. **A bricklay pattern is used to set diminishing volume:**
    >> Cylindrical rollers:
    >> 1½x underdirected
    >> 1½x half-off base
    >> 1½x off base

14. **Part and apply first row 1½x underdirected.**

15. **Part and apply next row 1½x half-off base:**
    >> Diameter of roller corresponds to diameter of rollers used to set expanded oval
    >> Work from center to either side
    >> Stagger bases to avoid splits

16. **Part and apply remaining lengths 1½x off base:**
    >> Set rollers on each side on angles to blend with curvature movement from expanded ovals

DRY HAIR

17. **Dry hair thoroughly under dryer:**
    >> Once dried, allow hair to cool; then remove all tools
    >> Drying time will vary according to hair length and density, and is not included in suggested salon speed

FINISH — COMB-OUT

18. **Relax set using your fingers:**
    >> Rake through hair
    >> Do not comb or brush hair at this point

19. Define and detail design:

>> Apply a silicone-based shine product
>> Use your fingers to arrange hair for a loose, tousled effect

□

20. The finish shows volume moving away from face blending to loose curls:

>> The expanded oval movement can be more or less apparent in the finished design depending on the finishing techniques chosen and the length of hair.

□

21. Optional: You may choose to relax set more fully and backcomb to blend bases.

□

COMPLETION

>> Discard single-use supplies
>> Disinfect tools and multi-use supplies
>> Disinfect workstation and arrange in proper order

□

30 mins
Suggested Salon Speed

My Speed
_____
_____
_____

INSTRUCTIONS:

Record your time in comparison with the suggested salon speed. Then, list here how you could improve your performance.

_____
_____
_____
_____
_____

ALTERNATING OBLONGS
ROLLERS AND PINCURLS

EXPLORE

How do you think waves can be created on straight hair?

INSPIRE

Learning to set alternating oblongs allows you to create wave patterns.

ACHIEVE

Following this *Alternating Oblongs – Rollers and Pincurls Workshop*, you'll be able to:

>> Create a wave pattern that moves away from the face and sides, blending to curly texture

>> Set and comb-out an alternating wave pattern with rollers

>> Set and comb-out an alternating skip wave pattern with curvature volume and indentation pincurls

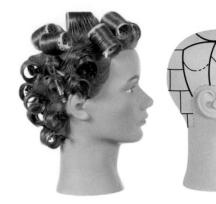

Alternating waves move away from the face and blend into the activated texture in the back.

Rollers are set in alternating volume oblongs at the top moving away from the front hairline.

At the sides, skip waves are set with volume pincurls followed by indentation pincurls. The oblongs blend into a bricklay pattern set with straight volume pincurls in the back.

WET-SETTING PROCEDURES –
ALTERNATING OBLONGS – ROLLERS AND PINCURLS

ALTERNATING OBLONGS – ROLLERS

ALTERNATING OBLONGS – PINCURLS

1. DISTRIBUTE:
   Convex – 1st direction
   Concave – 2nd direction

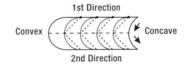

2. MOLD:
   Curved parallel

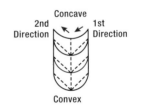

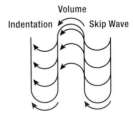

3. SCALE:
   Top: Volume oblongs
   Sides: Skip wave/volume | Indentation

4. PART:
   45° angle, rhomboid-shaped bases
   Volume pincurls: 1st direction
   Indentation pincurls: 2nd direction

5. APPLY:
   Curvature volume rollers: 1x half-off
   Curvature volume and indentation pincurls

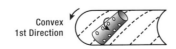

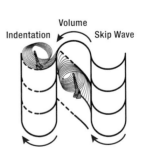

DESIGN DECISIONS CHART

ALTERNATING OBLONGS – ROLLERS AND PINCURLS

Draw or fill in the boxes with the appropriate answers.

DESIGN DECISIONS

STRUCTURE	FORM/TEXTURE		
DISTRIBUTE			
MOLD/SCALE			
PART/APPLY			
FINISH/DIRECTION			

Instructor Signature _____ **Date** _____

ALTERNATING OBLONGS
ROLLERS AND PINCURLS

View the video, complete the Design Decisions chart, then perform this workshop. Complete the self-check as you progress through the workshop.

40 mins
Suggested Salon Speed

PREPARATION		✔
	>> Assemble tools and products >> Set up workstation	☐

TOP – ALTERNATING OBLONGS – ROLLERS

	1. **Volume alternating oblongs are set on top with trapezoid-shaped bases.**	
	2. **Distribute, mold and scale a horizontal, counterclockwise oblong:** >> Apply styling gel evenly through clean, wet hair >> Distribute hair in 1st direction 45° toward convex end >> Mold 2nd direction toward concave end >> Scale oblong using length of roller with small end positioned in 1st direction	☐
	3. **Part first volume oblong beginning at convex end:** >> Measure 1x base size with large diameter of cone-shaped roller >> Part 45° angle with 1st direction to establish rhomboid-shaped base >> Project and distribute hair 90° from center of base	☐
	4. **Apply cone-shaped roller with small end toward point of origin:** >> Position roller half-off base parallel to the part >> Secure at small end of roller	☐

5. **Part and apply remainder of shape using same procedures:**
   >> 1x half-off base
   >> Secure at small end of roller

6. **Mold and scale second oblong in opposite direction moving clockwise.**

7. **Part and apply volume oblong beginning at convex end:**
   >> Part 45° angle in 1st direction
   >> 1x base size; rhomboid-shaped base
   >> 90° projection
   >> Half-off base
   >> Secure at small end of roller

8. **Complete second oblong using same procedures.**

9. **Mold, scale, part and apply last volume oblong in a counterclockwise direction using same procedures.**

SIDES — SKIP WAVES — VOLUME AND INDENTATION PINCURLS

10. **Alternating oblongs are set with pincurls on sides:**
    >> First oblong is molded (skipped)
    >> Second oblong is set with volume pincurls
    >> Third oblong is set with indentation pincurls

11. Mold and scale a skip wave:

>> Mold first oblong (concave end is positioned at top)
>> Mold and scale second oblong (volume)
>> Clips may be used to avoid disturbing first oblong

12. Part and apply curvature volume pincurls:

>> Begin at convex end
>> Part in a curved degree in 1st direction
>> Reinforce arc and form volume pincurl
>> Position circle half-off base
>> Secure in the 1st direction
>> Repeat until you complete oblong

13. Mold, scale, part and apply indentation pincurls:

>> Begin at concave end
>> Part from center of shape in 2nd direction
>> Turn ends up and away and form a circle
>> Position circle in upper portion of base
>> Secure in 2nd direction

14. Repeat same procedures on the opposite side:

>> First oblong is molded (skipped)
>> Second oblong is set with volume pincurls
>> Third oblong is set with indentation pincurls

BACK – BRICKLAY – STRAIGHT VOLUME PINCURLS

15. The bricklay pattern and horizontal partings are used to set straight volume pincurls in back.

16. Part and apply straight volume pincurls:

>> Distribute and mold hair downward
>> Measure base size relative to roller
>> Form a straight volume pincurl
>> Position and secure circle 1x half-off base
>> Stagger bases to avoid splits
>> Repeat until you complete bricklay pattern

DRY HAIR ✔

17. **Dry hair thoroughly under dryer:**
   >> Once dried, allow hair to cool; then remove all tools
   >> Drying time will vary according to hair length and density, and is not included in suggested salon speed

FINISH — COMB-OUT

18. **Relax set using one or two cushion brushes:**
   >> Begin in nape and work upward toward front hairline

19. **Dry mold in direction of set following the lines of the set.**

20. **Backbrush hair at top in direction of set using one-stroke technique.**

21. **Retrace and smooth lines of design in top area.**

22. Backbrush sides and back to blend to top.

23. Define lines of shape at sides:
>> Use a large-tooth comb to separate and detail activated texture

24. The finished design reveals alternating waves moving away from the face and sides and blending to the activated texture.

COMPLETION

>> Discard single-use supplies
>> Disinfect tools and multi-use supplies
>> Disinfect workstation and arrange in proper order

40 mins
Suggested Salon Speed

My Speed
_____
_____
_____

INSTRUCTIONS:
Record your time in comparison with the suggested salon speed. Then, list here how you could improve your performance.

_____
_____
_____
_____
_____

FINGERWAVING
AND MOLDING

EXPLORE //

What era is best known for making fingerwaves an iconic hairstyle?

ACHIEVE //

Following this lesson on *Fingerwaving and Molding,* you'll be able to:

>> Describe the process of creating fingerwaves

>> Explain how to create a skip wave

>> Identify the benefits of hair wrapping

INSPIRE //

Learning to mold hair designs with your fingers and combs will help you develop coordination, dexterity and strength.

FOCUS //

FINGERWAVING AND MOLDING

Fingerwaves

Skip Waves

Hair Wrapping

107ᶜ.12 | FINGERWAVING AND MOLDING

The foundation of classic hair designs begins by molding wet hair into straight or curved lines. In this lesson, you'll discover creative techniques for moving and directing hair, using the most basic tools: your own fingers, a comb and setting lotion.

Refer to the *Hair Design Skills* lesson for more on wet design theory.

FINGERWAVES

Fingerwaving is the art of shaping and defining the hair in graceful waves. This S-shaped wave pattern is a feminine style developed in the 1920s. Modern versions of fingerwaves continue to be worn today. Fingerwaves can be the complete design. Or, fingerwaves can be combined with pincurls–or with scrunching techniques–to create contrasting textures.

Learning to fingerwave will help you develop:

» Finger dexterity

» Hand/eye coordination

» Hand strength

Understanding the fingerwaving technique will increase your ability to visualize wave patterns on the curves of the head and create balanced designs.

A fingerwave is created by molding two complete alternating oblongs (shapings) that are joined and connected by a ridge. An overview of the technique is shown below. Refer to the *Fingerwaves and Flat Pincurls Workshop* for the complete step-by-step procedure.

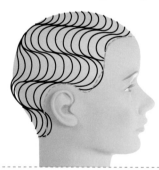  

The first step in designing fingerwaves is to plan the direction of the wave pattern. Waves can move horizontally, diagonally or vertically across the head. They can be designed with or without a part, move on or off the face and they can vary is size within a single design.

Oblongs may be created in a clockwise or counterclockwise direction, and they can be molded into a series of equal or unequal curved lines.

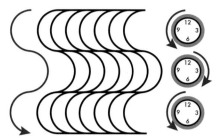 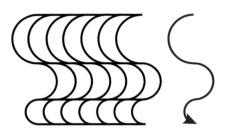

FINGERWAVING TECHNIQUE

1st Direction

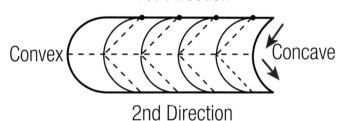

Convex — Concave

2nd Direction

Oblong shapes are the foundation of wave patterns. Important reference points include the concave or open end, and the convex or closed end. Think of a C shape divided in half. The upper half is the 1st direction and the lower half is the 2nd direction. A completed oblong creates a series of parallel curved lines.

SALONCONNECTION
Product Knowledge

Using the appropriate quantity and quality of hair care products will help ensure predictable results. The term Product Knowledge, or PK, is used by manufacturers to refer to the important information and advice for their products. Become familiar with products by reading about them and using them on your own hair and your friends' hair. Learn about products by using them on your mannequins too! Knowing which product to choose and how much to use, is a professional skill that is acquired by experience.

The following are key points to keep in mind while fingerwaving. Once setting lotion is applied to clean hair, it is distributed in the direction of the design. In the example below, the hair is distributed from a side part.

MOLD FIRST OBLONG

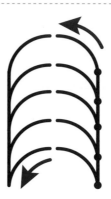

>> Mold 1st direction toward convex end.

>> Work from convex to concave end.

>> Mold 2nd direction toward concave end.

>> Work from concave to convex end.

>> Press down firmly in the center of the oblong with your finger as you mold.

>> Continue molding the 2nd direction until you reach the end of the first oblong.

ESTABLISH RIDGE AND BEGIN SECOND OBLONG

>> Begin ridge at concave end.

>> Postion teeth of comb along your index finger and slide comb approximately 1" (2.5 cm) toward the concave end.

>> Flatten comb, switch fingers to position ridge between your index finger and middle finger.

>> Turn comb, hold the ridge and distribute the hair in the opposite direction.

>> Roll your fingers forward, off the ridge to reinforce.

>> The 1st direction of the next oblong is established as the ridge is created.

>> Continue to distribute the 1st direction of the second oblong around the head. Mold the 2nd direction.

>> Repeat the process to establish the next ridge.

> Each wave movement consists of a hollow (recess) area and a ridge (high ledge). Pinching or pushing the ridge will create overdirection of the wave and is not recommended. Fingerwaves with low ridges are known as shadow waves.

2-COMB TECHNIQUE

Two combs can be used to create small narrow waves with strong ridges. In this technique, combs are used to hold and mold the hair in place of your fingers. Molding with two combs can be performed on all hair types, and is particularly effective on tightly curled hair textures.

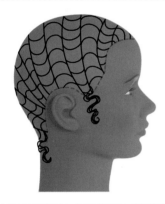

DISCOVER**MORE**

In the 1920s the bob hairstyle was trending with female celebrities and women in the workplace. Fingerwaves were developed as a way to style and soften that era's popular bob and quickly became popular with the women known as "flappers." This iconic vintage style is used today, with a modern twist, but the foundation to create fingerwaves remains the same. Search the Internet to see additional ways to create modern versions of fingerwaves.

SKIP WAVES

Skip waves are a variation of fingerwaves. **Skip waves are composed of two alternating oblongs connected by a ridge, with the first oblong molded and the second oblong set.**

>> One oblong is molded (skipped).

>> One oblong is set with pincurls, rollers or a round brush.

The oblong that is set supports the molded shape and gives more dimension to the design.

An alternation consisting of at least two oblongs and two rows of pincurls creates a skip wave and produces a strong wave pattern. Skip waves achieve wide, deep-flowing waves that are generally positioned on the side of the head, either diagonally or vertically. **One oblong followed by a row of pincurls is called a ridge curl.**

CREATING A SKIP WAVE

>> Mold two alternating oblongs with a connecting ridge.

>> Set flat pincurls in the second oblong.

>> Begin setting at the open or concave end.

>> Part in a curved line in the 2nd direction. Do not disturb the 1st direction.

>> Smooth and ribbon the hairstrand.

>> Form a flat pincurl.

>> Do not disturb the shapes or the ridge as you position and secure the pincurl with a clip.

>> Complete the row of pincurls.

>> Mold two more oblongs.

>> Leave the first oblong undisturbed and set the second in pincurls.

>> Dry the hair completely before combing this pattern out.

Optional: Indentation pincurls, rollers or a round brush can also be incorporated in the set oblong.

HAIR WRAPPING

Hair wrapping is a molding technique that is based on wrapping hair over the curves of the head. Wrapping creates smooth, straighter hair with a slight bend that reflects the curves of the head. Molding or wrapping the hair creates little to no volume since the hair is not lifted at the scalp. If volume is desired, rollers can be positioned in the crown area.

Hair wrapping can be performed on:

>> Wet hair

>> Dry hair

>> Relaxed hair

>> Curly hair

 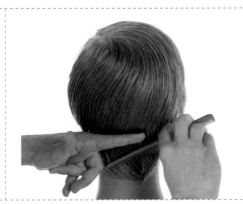 

Hair wrapping can be done from a side part or a single point of origin. It can be used to create the finished texture or as a foundation for another service such as blow drying or a curling iron technique.

CIRCLE WRAP

The circle wrap starts with distributing the hair from a single point of origin. The hair is molded section by section around the curves of the head. The hair is stretched while wet, then dried to create sleek, straight hair with less heat damage from stretching with a brush and blow dryer or the heat from a thermal iron. Once the hair is thoroughly dried, it is combed into the final design. Further finishing may be needed to touch up the design, such as using the flat iron in selected areas or adding curl to the ends of the hair.

Clients may dry wrap their hair as a "nighttime routine" to maintain their smooth, straight hair. By doing so, when they awaken in the morning and release their wrap, they have preserved the smooth texture. Much better than bed head!

Refer to the *Circle Wrap Workshop* for a complete step-by-step procedure.

Learning to mold and design wet hair with your fingers and a comb increases your ability to style hair in a variety of ways. You'll also build your finger dexterity, hand/ eye coordination and hand strength.

LESSONS LEARNED

To create a fingerwave:

>> Mold the 1st direction toward the closed end of an oblong shape.

>> Mold the 2nd direction by positioning your index finger in the center of the shape and molding toward the open end.

>> Create the ridge by positioning the teeth of the comb along your index finger and sliding the comb toward the concave end of the oblong.

>> Flatten the comb, switch fingers to position the ridge between your index and middle fingers; turn comb and distribute hair in the opposite direction to complete the ridge.

>> Repeat same procedures to complete fingerwave pattern.

To create a skip wave:

>> Mold two oblongs with a connecting ridge.

>> Set flat pincurls in the second oblong. Begin setting at the open or concave end. Do not disturb the shapes or the ridge as you position the pincurls.

>> Complete the row of pincurls. Mold two more oblongs. Leave the first oblong undisturbed and set the second.

Hair wrapping is a technique based on molding the hair over the curves of the head. Wrapping creates smooth, straighter hair with a slight bend that reflects the curves of the head. It can be used on:

>> Wet hair
>> Dry hair
>> Relaxed hair
>> Curly hair

Benefits of hair wrapping include achieving smooth, straight hair and a slight curve, while avoiding stretching wet hair and heat from a blow dryer, or applying excessive heat with thermal irons.

FINGERWAVES AND FLAT PINCURLS

EXPLORE

What shape(s) could you combine to create an "S" pattern?

INSPIRE

Learning the art of fingerwaving will allow you to create beautiful waves within any design.

ACHIEVE

Following this *Fingerwaves and Flat Pincurls Workshop*, you'll be able to:

>> Create a fingerwave design from a side part, finished with flat pincurls

>> Mold alternating oblongs with defined ridges to create fingerwaves

>> Set flat pincurls within alternating oblongs

Fingerwaves off a side part blend to activated texture resulting in expansion throughout the exterior.

Alternating oblongs are molded from a side part. Flat pincurls are set in the exterior.

WET-SETTING PROCEDURES – FINGERWAVES AND FLAT PINCURLS

FINGERWAVES   PINCURLS

1. DISTRIBUTE:
   Convex – 1st direction │ Concave – 2nd direction

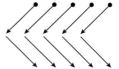

2. MOLD:
   Curved parallel lines │ Alternating oblongs

3. SCALE: N/A

4. PART:
   Flat pincurls: Concave end │ 2nd direction

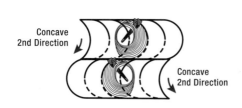

Concave
2nd Direction

Concave
2nd Direction

5. APPLY: Flat pincurls

FINGERWAVES AND FLAT PINCURLS

Draw or fill in the boxes with the appropriate answers.

DESIGN DECISIONS

STRUCTURE	FORM/TEXTURE		
DISTRIBUTE			
MOLD/SCALE			
PART/APPLY			
FINISH/DIRECTION			

Instructor Signature _____   **Date** _____

FINGERWAVES AND FLAT PINCURLS

View the video, complete the Design Decisions chart, then perform this workshop. Complete the self-check as you progress through the workshop.

35 mins
Suggested
Salon Speed

PREPARATION ✔

	>> Assemble tools and products >> Set up workstation	☐

DISTRIBUTE AND MOLD – FINGERWAVES

1. **Oblongs are molded to create fingerwaves:**

   >> 1st direction – 45° toward convex end
   >> 2nd direction – 45° toward concave end

2. **Distribute hair diagonally away from face to prepare for first oblong:**

   >> Apply gel evenly through wet hair
   >> Begin on heavy side of part at crown
   >> Work toward front hairline

   ☐

3. **Mold first oblong:**

   >> Begin at convex end
   >> Use fine teeth of molding comb
   >> Reinforce 1st direction (45°) using parallel curved distribution
   >> Position index finger firmly in center of shape to avoid disturbing 1st direction

   ☐

4. **Work toward concave end to complete 1st direction using same techniques.**

   Note: 2nd direction begins to form as a result of molding 1st direction.

   ☐

5. **Reinforce 2nd direction beginning at concave end:**
>> Position index finger firmly in center of shape to avoid disturbing 1st direction
>> Distribute hair 45° toward concave end
>> Work towards convex end

6. **Create ridge of first oblong:**
>> Begin at concave end
>> Use index finger to protect first oblong
>> Slide large teeth of comb approximately 1" (2.5 cm) toward concave end

7. **Reinforce ridge:**
>> Flatten comb and reposition index and middle finger to control ridge (avoid pinching ridge)
>> Turn comb upright and distribute lengths in opposite direction
>> Use fine teeth of comb to refine distribution
>> Keep palm off head to avoid disturbing oblong and ridge

   Note: 1st and 2nd direction of the second oblong begin to partially form.

8. **Complete ridge working toward convex end using same procedures.**

9. **The second oblong is molded around entire head:**
>> Avoid overdirecting hair at crown area

10. Continue to mold second oblong:

>> Distribute hair in 1st direction
>> Pivot through crown area
>> Work toward front hairline to complete 1st direction

11. Reinforce 2nd direction beginning at concave end:

>> Use index finger to protect 1st direction
>> Distribute 45° toward concave end
>> Work around crown and toward front hairline

12. Create ridge for second oblong:

>> Begin at concave end
>> Slide large teeth of comb toward concave end
>> Flatten comb and reposition index and middle fingers to protect ridge
>> Distribute lengths in opposite direction

13. Continue to create ridge working toward convex end:

>> Keep palm off hair to avoid disturbing oblong and ridge

14. Mold next alternating oblong:

>> Reinforce 1st direction
>> Mold 2nd direction

15. Create ridge of third oblong:

>> Begin at concave end using same techniques
>> Strive for equally spaced waves throughout design
>> Work toward convex end
>> Complete fingerwave pattern and prepare for pincurls

MOLD/SCALE/PART/APPLY – FLAT PINCURLS

16. Flat pincurls are set in nape within alternating oblongs.

17. Mold next alternating oblong:

>> Begin at concave end
>> Curved parallel distribution
>> Do not scale oblong to avoid disturbing ridge

18. Part a curved base in 2nd direction from center of shape:

>> Avoid disturbing 1st direction or ridge

Note: A tail comb is used to part and create the pincurls.

19. Create a flat pincurl and secure:

>> Form a smooth circle
>> Position circle in front of base within oblong shape
>> Secure in 2nd direction

	✔

20. Set remaining shape with flat pincurls using same techniques:

>> Pincurls will slightly overlap one another
>> Keep circles a consistent diameter

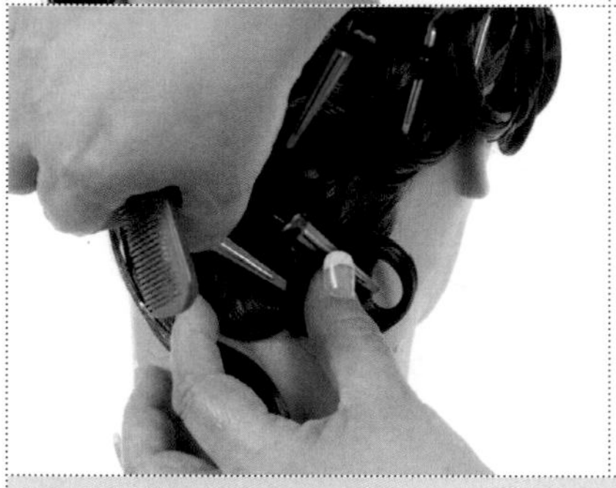

21. Set flat pincurls in last alternating oblong:

>> Begin at concave end
>> Part from center of shape in 2nd direction
>> Position circle in front of base
>> Secure in 2nd direction

DRY HAIR

22. Dry hair thoroughly under dryer:

>> Once dried, allow hair to cool; then remove clips
>> Drying time will vary according to hair length and density and is not included in suggested salon speed

FINISH — COMB-OUT

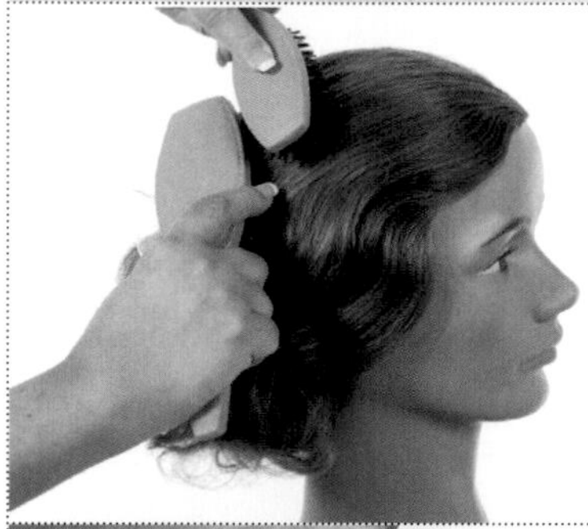

23. Relax set with cushion brush(es):

>> Begin at nape and work toward front hairline

24. Define form using wide-tooth tail comb:

>> Reinforce waves by moving comb and your fingers in alternating directions

		✓
	25. Lift hair along perimeter to separate ends and create additional expansion.	☐
	26. Long hairpins and holding spray may be used to reinforce wave movements.	☐
	27. The finish shows soft, undulating waves blending to activated texture along the perimeter.	☐

COMPLETION

		✓
	>> Discard single-use supplies >> Disinfect tools and multi-use supplies >> Disinfect workstation and arrange in proper order	☐

35 mins
Suggested Salon Speed

My Speed
_____
_____
_____

INSTRUCTIONS:

Record your time in comparison with the suggested salon speed. Then, list here how you could improve your performance.

_____

_____

_____

_____

_____

VARIATION — FINGERWAVES — 2-COMB TECHNIQUE

A variation on the fingerwaves using a 2-comb technique is available online.

CIRCLE WRAP

EXPLORE

What do you think of when you hear the term "wrap"?

INSPIRE

The curves of the head, a comb, your fingers and styling product are all you need to create silky hair designs.

ACHIEVE

Following this *Circle Wrap Workshop*, you'll be able to:

>> Create a smooth, silky finish by molding and wrapping the hair in a circular pattern

>> Mold a clockwise circle from a point of origin

The finish displays smooth, silky hair that frames the face.

Radial distribution is used from a point of origin just behind the apex. The hair is molded in a circular, clockwise direction.

WET-SETTING PROCEDURE – CIRCLE WRAP

1. DISTRIBUTE:
    Radial

    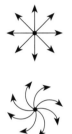

2. MOLD:
    Curved radial

3-5. SCALE/PART/APPLY:
    N/A

DESIGN DECISIONS CHART

CIRCLE WRAP

Draw or fill in the boxes with the appropriate answers.

DESIGN DECISIONS

STRUCTURE	FORM/TEXTURE		
DISTRIBUTE			
MOLDING PATTERN			
FINISH/DIRECTION			

Instructor Signature _____ **Date** _____

CIRCLE WRAP

View the video, complete the Design Decisions chart, then perform this workshop. Complete the self-check as you progress through the workshop.

20 mins
Suggested
Salon Speed

PREPARATION		✔
	>> Assemble tools and products >> Set up workstation	☐

DISTRIBUTE AND MOLD — INTERIOR

	1. Shampoo, towel-dry hair and apply a liberal amount of setting lotion: >> Take partings to apply product throughout hair >> Distribute product with a fine-tooth comb from base to ends	☐
	2. Section hair to establish point of origin: >> 4 quadrants >> Front hairline to center nape >> Behind apex to each ear	☐
	3. Distribute hair from point of origin using straight radial distribution: >> Position your finger on point of origin >> Begin in front-left quadrant >> Use tail of comb to draw radial lines from point of origin >> Repeat throughout all remaining quadrants	☐
	4. Refine direction of radial distribution prior to molding: >> Retrace lines of radial distribution	☐

5. Curved radial distribution is molded from point of origin.

6. **Mold circle in a clockwise direction:**
   >> Begin in back-left quadrant
   >> Protect point of origin by placing your index finger approximately 1" (2.5 cm) away
   >> Maintain tension to keep hair smooth and controlled

7. **Continue to mold circle:**
   >> Use your fingers to avoid disturbing previously molded hair
   >> Follow and blend lines to previously molded hair

8. **Direct lengths at front up and along front hairline:**
   >> Keep hair off face and continue to maintain tension

9. **Distribute hair from behind left ear upward:**
   >> Subdivide hair for control
   >> Mold and blend lengths to previously molded hair

10. **Use tip of tail comb to direct lengths up and around face:**
    >> Incorporate lengths into previously molded hair
    >> Use index finger to support molded direction

11. Mold hair following hairline down on opposite side:

>> Lift sideburn lengths around ear using tip of tail comb

DISTRIBUTE AND MOLD — EXTERIOR

12. Exterior is molded and blended into previously molded hair:

>> Clockwise direction
>> Follow curve of head

13. Continue to mold hair from back to above ear:

>> Use tip of tail comb to direct lengths over ear while using your finger to control molded lengths

14. Continue to reinforce molded clockwise direction:

>> Apply tension
>> Reinforce with index finger

15. Distribute and mold until all hair is smoothly incorporated.

16. Refine the circular molding:

>> Use tail comb lightly on surface

DRY HAIR ✓

17. Dry hair thoroughly under dryer:

>> Once dried, allow hair to cool; then remove paper strip
>> Drying time will vary according to hair length and density, and is not included in suggested salon speed

Optional: Position a paper strip around the hairline to keep the hair in place while under the hood dryer.

FINISH — COMB-OUT

18. Apply a shine spray to loosen the set.

19. Loosen surface using your fingers to ensure hair has dried completely while still molded.

20. Relax set following direction of wrap with tail comb.

21. Distribute hair into final finished direction using large-tooth tail comb.

	22. Define form and detail texture of design with tip of tail comb.	☐
	23. The result of the circle wrap features smooth, silky lengths that conform to the head and frame the face.	☐

COMPLETION

	>> Discard single-use supplies >> Disinfect tools and multi-use supplies >> Disinfect workstation and arrange in proper order	☐

20 mins
Suggested Salon Speed

My Speed
_____
_____
_____

INSTRUCTIONS:

Record your time in comparison with the suggested salon speed. Then, list here how you could improve your performance.

_____

_____

_____

_____

_____

EXPLORE //

What do glassblowing and welding have in common with thermal hair designing?

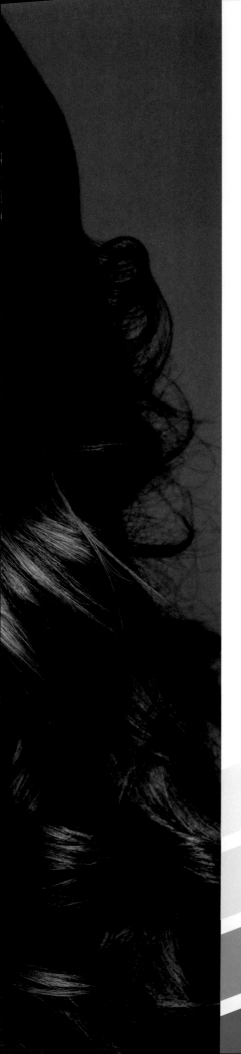

THERMAL DESIGN | 107^c.15

INSPIRE //

Your thermal design skills can provide the finishing touch to salon services you perform.

ACHIEVE //

Following this lesson on *Thermal Design,* you'll be able to:

>> Describe the three common ways to air form the hair

>> Contrast the various curling iron techniques

>> Summarize hair pressing

FOCUS //

THERMAL DESIGN

Air Forming

Thermal Ironing

Hair Pressing

107ᶜ.15 | THERMAL DESIGN

Thermal designing is the technique of drying and/or designing hair by using a hand-held dryer while simultaneously using your fingers, a variety of brushes, pressing combs and/or thermal irons.

Thermal means relating to or caused by heat. It is important to remember that heat is a form of energy that needs to be handled with great care, especially when used on hair. Thermal designing is sometimes referred to as thermal styling.

Blow dryers and thermal irons are the thermal tools available to the hair designer. Using these tools in conjunction with a variety of styling brushes and combs, you can achieve any number of creative and practical design solutions.

How does thermal designing really work to create temporary changes in texture and direction?

Hair is primarily composed of proteins connected by physical and chemical bonds.

HYDROGEN BONDS WEAKENED/ BROKEN DOWN	Hydrogen bonds are physical bonds that are weakened or broken by water or heat such as from a thermal service.
PROTEIN CHAINS SHIFT	When hydrogen bonds are weakened/broken down, protein chains are able to shift into a new, temporary position.
HYDROGEN BONDS REFORMED	After blow drying or thermal curling, the bonds are reformed into the new configuration as the hair cools—but only temporarily.

It is necessary to allow the hair to cool completely prior to brushing or combing.

>> If the hair is stretched while it is still warm, the bonds are still in a weakened state and the curl pattern will not hold.

Water will also break the new pattern. Hair will return to its original shape and curl configuration if it comes in contact with any of the following after a thermal design service:

>> Rain

>> Humidity

>> Shampooing

Position of Brush:

» Volume – Brush is positioned underneath the hairstrand, and the brush is rolled upward from ends-to-base

» Indentation – Brush is positioned on top of the hairstrand, and the brush is rolled upward from ends-to-base

When air forming for volume and indentation, keep in mind that it is the position, direction and continual motion of the brush that control the amount of volume or indentation achieved.

The more familiar you become with your tools, the more you'll interchange these tools to achieve the desired effects, even within the same design.

9-ROW BRUSH

VENT AND ROUND BRUSH

BOAR-BRISTLE ROUND BRUSH

Air Forming Tips

THERMAL-PROTECTANT PRODUCT	TOWEL-BLOT HAIR	PROGRESSIVE HEAT TEMPERATURES
Always use a thermal-protectant product before any air forming procedure to protect against damage and to: » Reduce friction » Form a clear, protective barrier against mechanical damage and drying effects of heat Excessive air forming can cause hair to lose elasticity or create split ends.	To save time and energy, remove approximately 90% of the water from the hair before designing: » Towel-blot to eliminate excess water Because water keeps the hydrogen bonds in a softened state, designing with heat at an overly wet stage is more difficult.	A progressive decrease in temperature helps smooth the transition from wet, slippery hair, to hair that is more fixed and formable: » Dry hair (90%) on high heat setting first » Switch to medium heat to design hair » Set design with cool air; use cool shot button to reduce warmth that curls retain Retained heat makes the curls pliable and they are likely to "fall" back to their natural bond formation.
AIRFLOW DIRECTION	DRYER DISTANCE	LIGHTENED (BLEACHED) OR CHEMICALLY RELAXED HAIR
Air form in the direction of the cuticle scales, not against them. Keep the dryer's airflow pointing down the hairstrand from the scalp to the ends to: » Protect scalp » Improve hair's sheen » Prevent frizziness	Reduce the potential of hair and scalp damage from heat by: » Always keeping dryer 3" to 5" (7.5 cm to 12.5 cm) from hair » Constantly moving dryer in a back-and-forth motion	Use additional caution and lower heat settings when drying lightened (bleached) or chemically relaxed hair, since it is even more susceptible to the drying effects of heat. Thermal protectant products are recommended along with regular conditioning treatments.

THERMAL IRONING

Thermal ironing involves a variety of tools that are used to impart various texture patterns on dry hair—from straight to curly to crimped.

Thermal irons include:
>> Curling irons
>> Flat (straightening) irons
>> Crimping irons
>> Undulating irons

CURLING IRONS

Thermal curling is the process of temporarily adding curl texture to dry hair using heated irons (electric or stove-heated). The earliest thermal irons were curling irons, first introduced by Marcel Grateau in 1875. These irons are now often called "marcel irons." Thermal waving or curling is achieved by applying heat to dry hair from either an electric or stove-heated curling iron to create curls or waves for a finished hair design. Curling irons are available in a variety of diameters, sizes, shapes and colors. The barrel and groove is made of stainless steel to retain heat.

PARTS OF A CURLING IRON

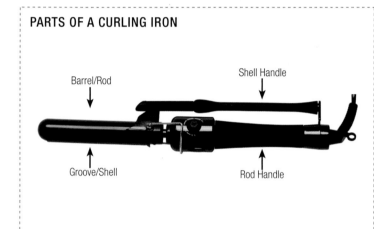

Barrel/Rod

Shell Handle

Groove/Shell

Rod Handle

Rod Handle
Electric curling irons have a swivel at the base of the handle that permits the electric cord to turn, without twisting, as the iron is being manipulated.

Barrel/Rod
Round, heating cylinder

Shell Handle
Controls the groove/shell

Groove/Shell
Clamp that holds the hair against the barrel

The electric curling iron contains a heating element controlled by a thermostat that maintains a constant temperature during use.

>> A good iron should be able to be left on for an entire day and still maintain the correct temperatures.

>> Never touch a curling iron with your fingers or place it near your nose to smell if it is hot.

>> Test an iron's heat by bringing your hand very near the barrel, without touching it. You can sufficiently judge the amount of heat an iron is giving off this way.

>> Metal curling iron holders retain heat. If you use a metal holder be sure to test the temperature of the iron before using it on your client's hair.

>> Lower temperatures are recommended for fine, chemically altered or lightened hair.

>> Close a hot iron lightly on a damp towel before curling porous, white or lightened (bleached) hair. This step is not necessary for most hair types, but some tinted hair and very fine hair will also benefit from testing and cooling the iron first. Proceeding with a lower iron temperature will prevent scorching or dryness. Test temperature prior to service to prevent scorching.

Holding a Curling Iron

Following are two ways you can open and close a curling iron:

1. Use little finger to open the iron, and the other fingers to close the iron.

2. Use little finger and ring finger to open the iron, and the other fingers to close the iron.

Practice Manipulations With the Curling Iron

Because curling irons can be difficult to use and can burn the hairstrand if used incorrectly, practice is recommended. Practice with a cold iron on your mannequin in the beginning until you are comfortable with the manipulations.

» Practice rolling the iron toward you (standing in back of your mannequin or client, this will be a downward rotation) while opening and closing the clamp at regular intervals.

   ■ As the iron is turned in downward circular movements, a swivel at the base of the handle will permit the iron to turn without twisting the cord.

   ■ As you continue to turn the iron, shift your thumb to aid in the turning motion.

» Practice rolling the iron away from you (standing in back of your mannequin or client, this will be an upward rotation) while opening and closing the clamp at regular intervals.

» Practice rolling the hair first in one direction, and then in another. End each curling rotation by releasing the hair, which is done by opening and closing the clamp in a quick "clicking" movement.

CLEANING THERMAL IRONS

It is important to keep your thermal irons clean for proper use.

» Run a fine-grade steel wool pad along the barrel of the iron while it is slightly warm to remove any styling residue.

» Clean the iron in the direction that the hair flows across the barrel to ensure that the hair will not flow against the grain and become damaged:

   ■ Move the wool pad around the circumference of the barrel, not vertically (base to tip)

   ■ Use only a gentle cleaning method on Teflon or other coatings. Do not use steel wool as it can chip and wear off the coating, leading to abrasion during use.

Thermal designing is a skill that will be requested by the majority of clients in the salon. Whether it is to complete another service or as a weekly or biweekly service, it is crucial that these skills are mastered to keep your clients coming back.

Curling Iron Techniques

Following are examples of different curling iron techniques and various texture patterns that can be achieved by varying the position of the curling iron along the hairstrand. Curling irons that are cylindrical in shape create a texture pattern that reflects their diameter.

>> For volume, position the barrel of the curling iron underneath the hairstrand.

>> For indentation, position the barrel of the curling iron on top of the hairstrand.

> Always feed the ends of the hair all the way through the curling iron to avoid crimped "fishhook" ends.

BASE-TO-ENDS TECHNIQUES

>> Creates volume and support at base and a consistent curl pattern throughout hair strand.

>> Hair positioned slightly away from base, then iron is turned ½ revolution at a time while feeding entire strand into iron

>> Can be used on shorter to longer lengths

>> Three types: Figure 4, Figure 6 and Figure 8

FIGURE 4
Good for shorter hair

FIGURE 6
Good for medium-length hair

FIGURE 8
Good for longer lengths

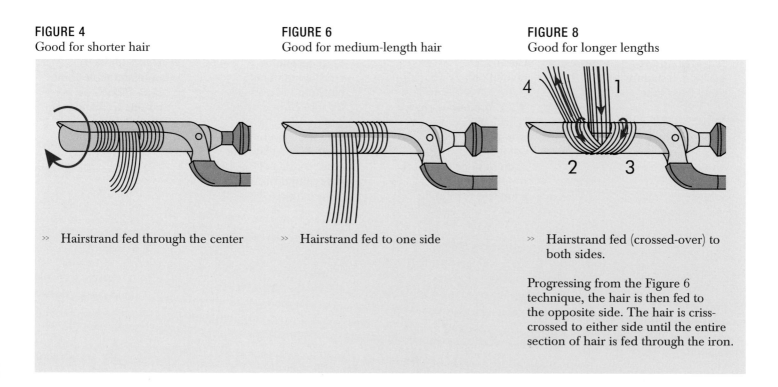

>> Hairstrand fed through the center

>> Hairstrand fed to one side

>> Hairstrand fed (crossed-over) to both sides.

Progressing from the Figure 6 technique, the hair is then fed to the opposite side. The hair is criss-crossed to either side until the entire section of hair is fed through the iron.

Following are tips for applying the **Figure 4** technique:

>> Barrel positioned underneath strand near the base

>> Ends are controlled with opposite hand

>> Ends of hair are directed through center

>> Curling iron is continually turned with quick "clicking" movements

>> Hard-rubber or nonflammable comb is positioned between curling iron and scalp to protect against accidental burning

Following are tips for applying the **Figure 6** technique:

>> Barrel of iron is positioned slightly away from base

>> Ends controlled with opposite hand

>> Curling iron turned ½ revolution toward scalp

>> With continuous quick "clicking" movements, iron is turned ½ revolution away from scalp in same direction, resulting in one complete revolution

>> Same technique repeated until entire hairstrand is gradually fed into curling iron

>> One hand continually controls lengths while other continually clicks and turns iron toward base

>> Hard-rubber or nonflammable comb is positioned between curling iron and scalp to protect against accidental burning

ENDS-TO-BASE TECHNIQUE

The ends-to-base technique is used to achieve stronger end curl, progressing to a weaker base.

» The curling iron is positioned at the ends of the hair and then rotated upward toward the base.

» With shorter hair, the curl reflects the diameter of the curling iron.

ENDS TECHNIQUE

The ends technique is used to achieve a curved under or bevel-up (flipped) effect.

» For volume, the curling iron is positioned underneath the strand and turned under for a curved-under effect.

» With indentation, the curling iron is positioned on top of the strand and turned upward for a bevel-up (flipped) effect.

MARCEL WAVES TECHNIQUE

A curling iron and comb are used to achieve an alternating wave pattern along the hairstrand, commonly referred to as marcel waves.

» The hairstrand is placed into the curling iron with the barrel positioned on top of the strand and the shell beneath the strand.

» The iron is then closed and a comb is used to encourage the direction of the hairstrand beneath the barrel of the iron.

» This technique is repeated in alternating directions to form the wave.

SPIRAL TECHNIQUE

The spiral technique is used to achieve elongated spiral curls or a corkscrew effect.

» The curling iron is positioned vertically or diagonally.

» Ends-to-base technique – Curling iron is positioned on the ends of the hair, then the iron is turned upward toward the base.

» Base-to-ends technique – Hairstrand is generally wound around the iron until the entire strand is fed through and the ends are within the iron. The hair can also be wound around the barrel of the iron in a corkscrew pattern.

FLAT (STRAIGHTENING) IRONS

Flat (straightening) irons consist of two flat plates. The hair is placed between the two heated flat plates near the base and then brought down to the ends in one smooth, flowing movement. This technique is referred to as straightening or silking the hair.

Flat iron techniques may be performed throughout the design to create a smooth finish, or in certain areas to achieve contrasting textures.

As you become proficient with the flat iron, you will find that wrapping the hairstrand around the iron or turning the flat iron in a circular motion along the hairstrand creates various types of curved textures or curls.

CRIMPING IRONS

Crimping irons are used to create an angular or zigzag pattern, which is often referred to as crimped hair.

>> Crimping irons consist of two plates that have an angular or serrated pattern.

>> The hair is positioned between the plates, which are then closed upon the hair.

>> Depending on the desired effect, crimped texture can be performed along the entire strand or in a specific area for a special effect.

UNDULATING IRONS

The undulating iron is used to create wavy textures along the hairstrand.

>> Undulating irons consist of two undulating or curved plates that create an "S" pattern. The hair is positioned between the plates, which are then closed upon the hair.

>> This technique can be performed throughout the entire design, or used in a specific area for a special effect.

HAIR PRESSING

Hair pressing, or **silking**, is a technique of temporarily straightening curly and tightly curled hair using a pressing comb or straightening iron.

>> First, the hair is shampooed and conditioned.

>> Next, the hair is air formed with a brush using tension to begin to reduce the natural curl pattern.

>> Then, a protective oil or cream is applied to the hair.

>> Finally, a hot pressing comb or straightening iron is used to further straighten and smooth the natural curl pattern. Generally, smaller sections of hair are used to achieve thorough pressing.

PRESSING COMBS

The pressing comb is used to apply heat and tension to temporarily straighten tightly curled hair. The pressing comb is used on completely dry hair. It is the pressing action of the heated spine of the comb against the hair that accomplishes the smooth effect.

There are two types of pressing combs made of stainless steel or brass:

>> Stove-heated pressing comb – Has a wooden handle since wood does not absorb heat and is heated in a "stove" or "stove heater"

>> Electric pressing comb – Has either an "on and off" switch or a thermostat with a control switch that allows the hair designer to select high or low heat settings

HAIR-PRESSING TECHNIQUES

The number of times you repeat the pressing action on the same subsection of hair depends on the amount of curl you wish to remove.

There are two techniques used in pressing:

1. **Soft press** – Pressing the hair once on each side with less pressure and heat

2. **Hard** or **double press** – Pressing the hair twice on each side with more pressure and heat

If hair is not getting as straight as desired, use more pressure and/or more heat.

Pressing Tips and Considerations

>> Hair pressing is considered less damaging to the structure of the hair in comparison to a chemical relaxer service; the hair is left with more strength and body.

>> Clients have more color options available when they select a temporary pressing service versus a chemical change.

>> Hair pressing results only last until the next shampoo.

>> Exposure to high humidity can cause curl patterns to revert back to the natural texture.

>> Various products such as pressing oils and creams can be used to prevent scorching and breakage during a pressing service and protect the hair overall.

Hair Texture

Because the pressing services can require the designer to heat the hair for a long period of time, analyzing the type, texture and condition of the hair is particularly important.

Fine	Medium	Coarse
>> Especially delicate and must be treated gently	>> Least difficult to press	>> Can be resistant
>> Less heat and pressure to avoid breakage	>> No particular precautions	>> Can tolerate more heat and pressure

>> Avoid pressing chemically damaged hair and pressing the hair too often, which can cause breakage.
>> Frequent conditioning of the hair will help protect against breakage, dry scalp, split ends and dull appearance.

PRESS AND CURL SERVICE

A press and curl service involves pressing the hair first and then curling or waving the hair with a thermal iron. This service provides additional texture options for clients who have naturally curly or tightly curled hair, and for those who wish to avoid a chemical relaxing service.

PRESSING		Dry hair is pressed, generally working from the nape to the front.
CURLING		Once the hair is pressed it is ready to be curled. » A marcel iron is used to curl the hair according to the desired results » Any curling iron technique may be used to include, base-to-ends, ends-to-base, or ends only
PRESS AND CURL FINISH		The finish shows a combination of textures that can be achieved through pressing and curling iron techniques.

ALERT!

Remember, burned hair cannot be reconditioned.

TESTING TEMPERATURE

It is important that you protect the hair from excessive heat.

» Most thermal design tools are manufactured so that the temperature is maintained at a level that is safe for the hair.

» **When working with stove-heated pressing combs or thermal irons, you'll need to check the temperature by testing the pressing comb or thermal iron on a piece of white paper towel. If the iron is too hot:**

■ **The paper towel turns yellow or brown, or scorches after about 5 seconds.**

■ **Allow the pressing comb or iron to cool a bit before using it on the hair.**

DISCOVER**MORE**

Purchasing Thermal Tools

When deciding which thermal tools to purchase, it's important for you to do your research. New tools enter the market frequently. Professional tools are designed to withstand hours of daily use, while consumer tools may only be used once a day. Keep in mind that thermal tools are an investment and even though the cost may seem high, they are worth the investment. It will pay off in your finished designs! Research terms used to describe thermal tools online such as ionic, ceramic, tourmaline or titanium.

LESSONS LEARNED

>> The three common ways to air form the hair include, fingerstyling, scrunching and air forming with a brush:

- Fingerstyling is a technique in which the fingers manipulate and design the hair as it's dried with the blow dryer.

- Scrunching, a form of fingerstyling, involves gently squeezing the hair lengths as the hair dries using a diffuser to introduce a texture pattern that the hair responds to naturally.

- Air forming with a blow dryer and a brush allows you to change the form, direction and texture.

>> Various curling iron techniques include:

- Base-to-ends – Creates volume and support at the base and a consistent curl pattern throughout the strand

- Ends-to-base – Achieves stronger end curl progressing to a weaker base

- Ends – Achieves a curved-under or bevel-up effect

- Marcel waves – Achieve an alternating wave pattern along the hairstrand using a curling iron and comb

- Spiral – Achieves elongated spiral curls or a corkscrew-effect

>> Hair pressing, or silking, is a way of temporarily straightening curly and tightly curled hair. The number of times the pressing action is performed on the same subsection of hair depends on the amount of curl to be removed:

- Soft press means pressing the hair once on each side with less pressure and heat

- Hard or double press means pressing the hair twice on each side with more pressure and heat

BEVEL-UNDER
AIR FORMING/ROUND BRUSH

EXPLORE

What tools can hairdressers use to curve the ends of the hair under?

INSPIRE

From short to medium to long, the bevel-under look is versatile on all lengths.

ACHIEVE

Following this *Bevel-Under – Air Forming/Round Brush Workshop*, you'll be able to:

>> Create a smooth design with the ends curved under by using straight volume air forming techniques with a round brush

Air forming straight volume on solid form lengths expands the form and adds fullness along the perimeter.

Straight volume is created with the use of horizontal partings, varying base controls, and medium- and large-diameter round brushes.

THERMAL SETTING PROCEDURES – BEVEL-UNDER – ROUND BRUSH

1-2. DISTRIBUTE/MOLD:
    Straight parallel

3-5. SCALE/PART/APPLY:
    Horizontal partings │ Rectangular bases │
    1x half-off base │ 1x off base │
    Straight volume bevel-under

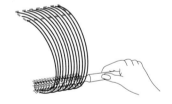

DESIGN DECISIONS CHART

BEVEL-UNDER – AIR FORMING/ROUND BRUSH

Draw or fill in the boxes with the appropriate answers.

DESIGN DECISIONS			
STRUCTURE	FORM/TEXTURE		
DISTRIBUTE/MOLD			
SCALE/PART/APPLY			
FINISH/DIRECTION			

Instructor Signature _____ **Date** _____

BEVEL-UNDER
AIR FORMING/ROUND BRUSH

View the video, complete the Design Decisions chart, then perform this workshop. Complete the self-check as you progress through the workshop.

20 mins
Suggested Salon Speed

PREPARATION		✔
	>> Assemble tools and products >> Set up workstation	☐

DISTRIBUTE/MOLD

	1. **Apply styling mousse to help create support:** >> Towel-dry hair >> Distribute product with fingers throughout hair	☐
	2. **Air form to remove excess moisture:** >> Use fingers or vent brush to control hair >> Direct airflow from base to end **Note:** A concentrator is not used at this time since direct airflow is not required.	☐

SCALE/PART/APPLY

	3. **Section with a side part:** >> Part above center of left eye to crown, crown to center nape	☐

4. **Air form hair using half-off base volume control from a horizontal parting:**

>> Attach a concentrator to blow dryer to help direct airflow
>> Position medium-diameter round brush underneath hair to create base lift
>> Direct airflow to follow cuticle of hair
>> Dry base, midstrand, then ends
>> Rotate brush upward from ends
>> Allow hair to cool before removing round brush
>> Work from center to each side

5. **Work upward using same air forming procedures:**

>> Take a small portion of previously air formed lengths to blend bases
>> Work from center to each side

6. **Reinforce curl on ends:**

>> Rotate brush toward base
>> Direct airflow over hair
>> Allow hair to cool before removing round brush

7. **Partings above ear extend to front hairline.**

8. **Work from center back to front hairline using off-base control:**

   » Switch to a larger diameter round brush on longer lengths

9. **Complete one side using same air forming procedures.**

10. **Repeat on opposite side and check for symmetry of the bevel-under.**

11. **Work toward top using same air forming procedures:**

    » Air form from center to either side to maintain symmetry

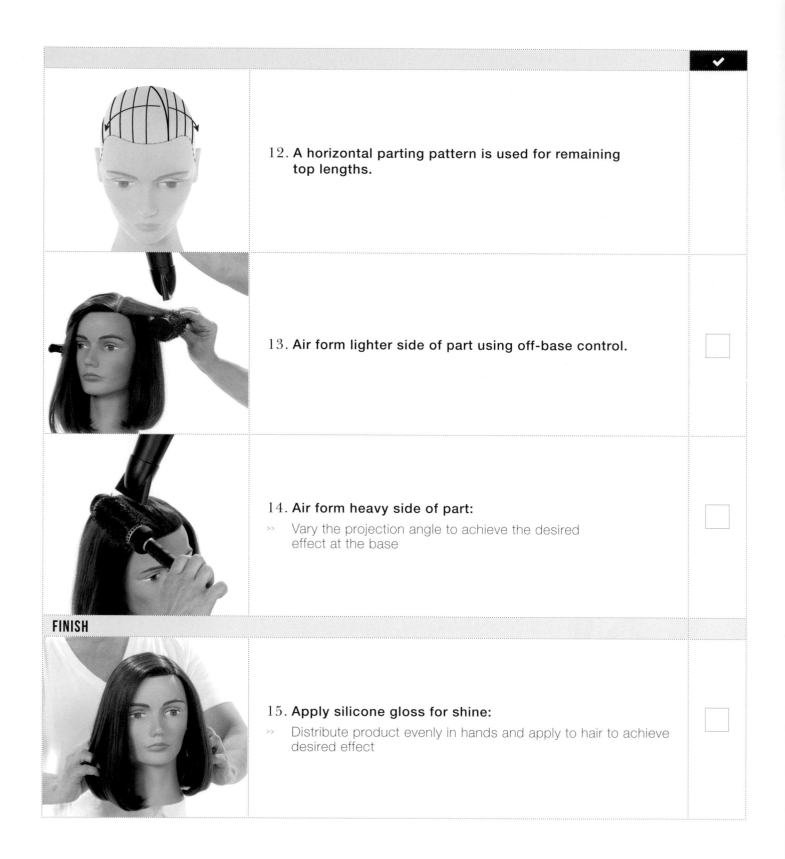

12. **A horizontal parting pattern is used for remaining top lengths.**

13. **Air form lighter side of part using off-base control.**

14. **Air form heavy side of part:**
    >> Vary the projection angle to achieve the desired effect at the base

FINISH

15. **Apply silicone gloss for shine:**
    >> Distribute product evenly in hands and apply to hair to achieve desired effect

16. **The finish shows a smooth surface with perimeter weight accentuated by end texture with a bevel-under effect.**

☐

COMPLETION

>> Discard single-use supplies
>> Disinfect tools and multi-use supplies
>> Disinfect workstation and arrange in proper order

☐

20 mins
Suggested Salon Speed

My Speed
_____
_____
_____

INSTRUCTIONS:

Record your time in comparison with the suggested salon speed. Then, list here how you could improve your performance.

_____

_____

_____

_____

_____

VARIATION — SOFT "FLIP" EFFECT

A variation on the round brush to create a soft "flip" effect using straight volume indentation techniques is available online.

FLAT IRON

EXPLORE

What are some professions that require tools to create a straight, flat, smooth surface?

INSPIRE

Flat-iron techniques temporarily straighten hair so clients can wear the unactivated styles they desire.

ACHIEVE

Following this *Flat Iron Workshop*, you'll be able to:

>> Create a design with a smooth, sleek finish from base-to-ends using flat-iron techniques

Flat-ironing the hair creates very straight, unactivated lengths with minimal volume.

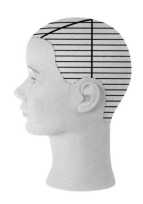

Horizontal partings are used throughout to air form and flat-iron the hair. An off-center parting creates an asymmetrical finish.

THERMAL SETTING PROCEDURES – FLAT IRON

1-2. DISTRIBUTE/MOLD:
Straight parallel

3-5. SCALE/PART/APPLY:
Horizontal partings | Rectangular-shaped bases | Straight volume

AIR FORM

FLAT IRON

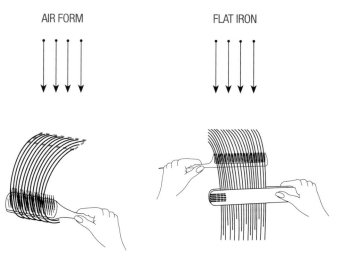

DESIGN DECISIONS CHART
FLAT IRON

Draw or fill in the boxes with the appropriate answers.

DESIGN DECISIONS

STRUCTURE	FORM/TEXTURE		
AIR-FORMING PATTERN			
FLAT IRONING PATTERN			
FINISH/DIRECTION			

Instructor Signature _____ **Date** _____

FLAT IRON

View the video, complete the Design Decisions chart, then perform this workshop. Complete the self-check as you progress through the workshop.

40 mins
Suggested
Salon Speed

PREPARATION		✔
	>> Assemble tools and products >> Set up workstation	☐

DISTRIBUTE/MOLD

	1. **Apply smoothing cream to soften lengths, create minimum hold and protect hair from heat styling:** >> Towel-dry hair >> Distribute cream throughout lengths from base-to-ends	☐

SCALE/PART/APPLY – AIR FORM

	2. **Air form to remove excess moisture:** >> Use fingers to control hair >> Direct airflow from base-to-ends **Note:** A concentrator is not used at this time since direct airflow is not required.	☐
	3. **Horizontal partings are used throughout to air form lengths in direction of design.**	

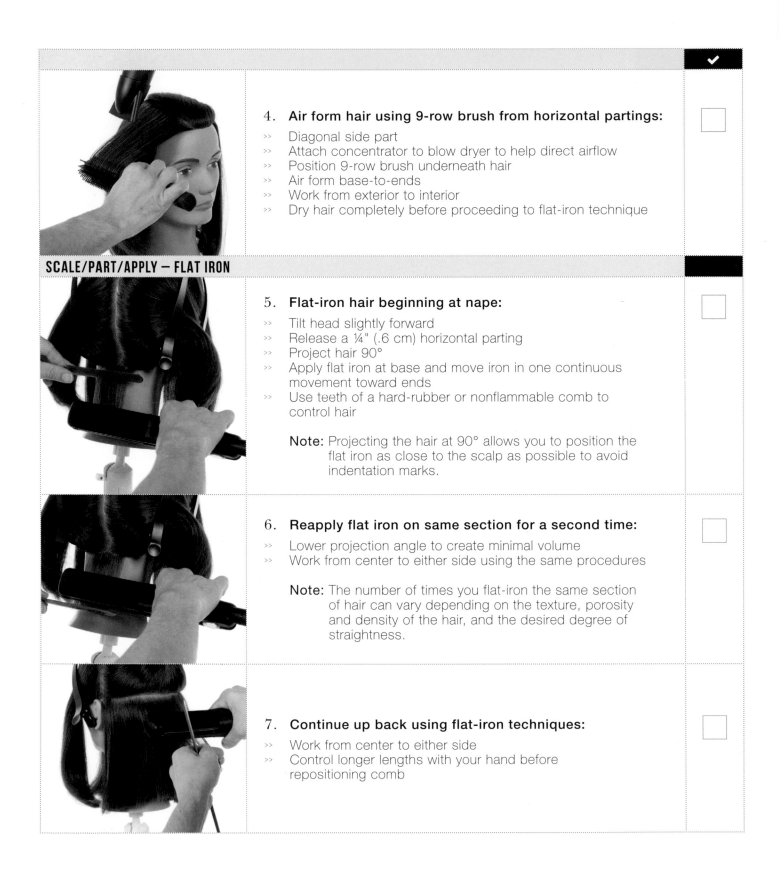

4. **Air form hair using 9-row brush from horizontal partings:**

>> Diagonal side part
>> Attach concentrator to blow dryer to help direct airflow
>> Position 9-row brush underneath hair
>> Air form base-to-ends
>> Work from exterior to interior
>> Dry hair completely before proceeding to flat-iron technique

SCALE/PART/APPLY – FLAT IRON

5. **Flat-iron hair beginning at nape:**

>> Tilt head slightly forward
>> Release a ¼" (.6 cm) horizontal parting
>> Project hair 90°
>> Apply flat iron at base and move iron in one continuous movement toward ends
>> Use teeth of a hard-rubber or nonflammable comb to control hair

Note: Projecting the hair at 90° allows you to position the flat iron as close to the scalp as possible to avoid indentation marks.

6. **Reapply flat iron on same section for a second time:**

>> Lower projection angle to create minimal volume
>> Work from center to either side using the same procedures

Note: The number of times you flat-iron the same section of hair can vary depending on the texture, porosity and density of the hair, and the desired degree of straightness.

7. **Continue up back using flat-iron techniques:**

>> Work from center to either side
>> Control longer lengths with your hand before repositioning comb

8. **Extend partings to front hairline once you reach ears and continue flat-iron techniques:**
   >> First at 90° to get close to base
   >> Second at lower projection angle to bring hair close to head and reduce volume

9. **Work up to crest area using same flat-iron techniques:**
   >> Project hair 90° to get close to base

10. **Reapply flat iron for a second time to direct lengths closer to head to reduce volume.**

11. **Work up to side parting using same flat-iron techniques:**
    >> Horizontal partings
    >> 90° projection
    >> Position flat iron as close to scalp as possible

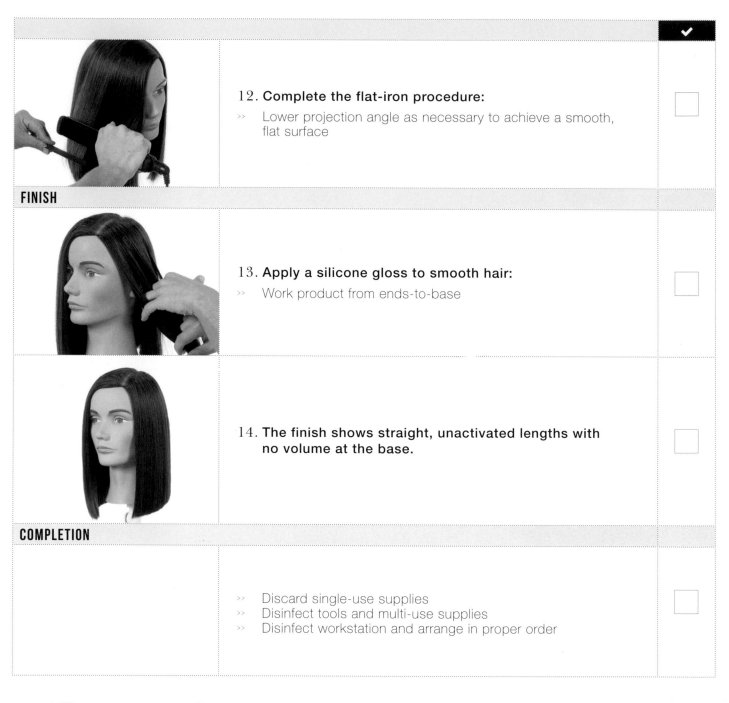

✔

12. **Complete the flat-iron procedure:**
   >> Lower projection angle as necessary to achieve a smooth, flat surface

FINISH

13. **Apply a silicone gloss to smooth hair:**
   >> Work product from ends-to-base

14. **The finish shows straight, unactivated lengths with no volume at the base.**

COMPLETION

   >> Discard single-use supplies
   >> Disinfect tools and multi-use supplies
   >> Disinfect workstation and arrange in proper order

40 mins
Suggested
Salon Speed

My Speed
_____
_____
_____

INSTRUCTIONS:
Record your time in comparison with the suggested salon speed. Then, list here how you could improve your performance.

_____
_____
_____
_____
_____

ROUND BRUSH AIR FORMING

EXPLORE

Why do you think blow dry bars are appealing to clients?

INSPIRE

Perfecting your air forming and round brush skills allows you to provide your clients with exceptional finished designs.

ACHIEVE

Following this *Round Brush Air Forming Workshop*, you'll be able to:

>> Create a progression of volume that moves away from the face using air forming techniques with a round brush

Directional volume air forming is used to create a progression of volume from exaggerated at the front hairline to diminished at the nape.

Horizontal, diagonal-forward and vertical partings are used to air form hair away from the face. Bases are staggered to avoid splits and encourage blending. A progression of base controls is used to create a progression of volume.

THERMAL-SETTING PROCEDURES – ROUND BRUSH AIR FORMING

1-2. DISTRIBUTE/MOLD:
Straight parallel

3-5. SCALE/PART/APPLY:

Partings
Horizontal │ Diagonal-forward │ Vertical

Rectangular bases
1x half-off base │ 1x on base │ 1½x overdirected

Staggered bases to avoid splits

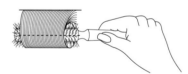

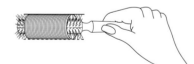

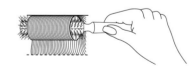

ROUND BRUSH AIR FORMING

Draw or fill in the boxes with the appropriate answers.

DESIGN DECISIONS

STRUCTURE

FORM/TEXTURE

DISTRIBUTE/MOLD

SCALE/PART/APPLY

FINISH/DIRECTION

Instructor Signature _____   Date _____

PERFORMANCE GUIDE

ROUND BRUSH AIR FORMING

View the video, complete the Design Decisions chart, then perform this workshop. Complete the self-check as you progress through the workshop.

25 mins
Suggested Salon Speed

PREPARATION		✔
	>> Assemble tools and products >> Set up workstation	☐

DISTRIBUTE/MOLD

	1. Air form to remove excess moisture: >> Distribute styling product >> Use vent brush to control hair >> Direct airflow from base to ends	☐

SCALE/PART/APPLY

	2. Horizontal, diagonal-forward and vertical partings are used within a staggered base pattern.	

	3. Air form lengths at nape from horizontal parting: >> Position round brush underneath hair and dry base, midstrand and ends >> Rotate brush in a continuous motion from ends to base to form curl >> Position brush half-off base >> Allow hair to cool before removing brush >> Work from center to either side	☐

4. **Air form lengths from diagonal-forward partings as you work upward:**
   >> Stagger bases to avoid splits

5. **Switch to on-base control at upper crown for maximum volume.**

6. **Air form hair from vertical partings as you work from top to either side:**
   >> Direct lengths away from face and position brush parallel to its base.

7. **Overdirect fringe for exaggerated volume:**
   >> 1½x base size
   >> Use airflow to direct lengths into brush

FINISH	✔

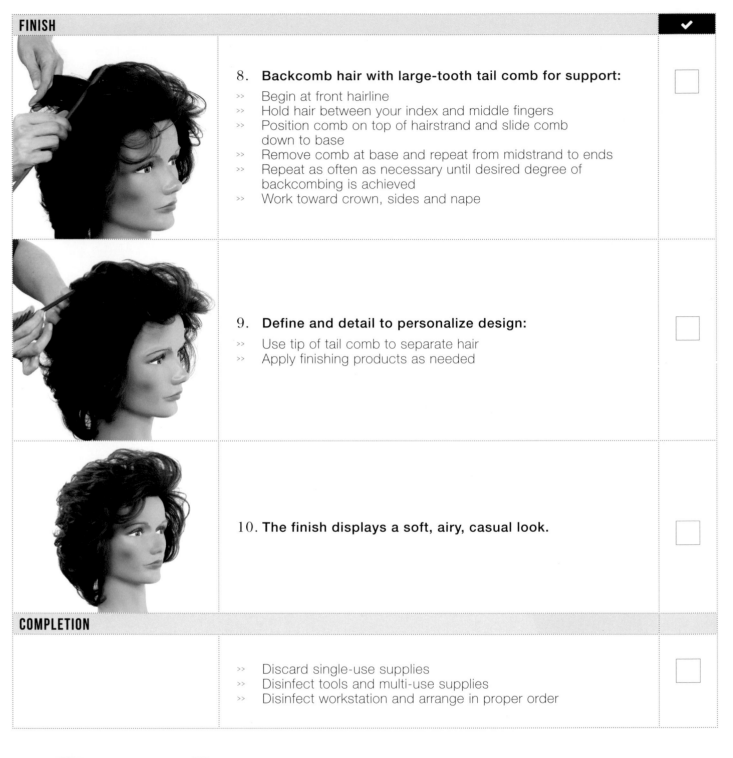

8. Backcomb hair with large-tooth tail comb for support:

» Begin at front hairline
» Hold hair between your index and middle fingers
» Position comb on top of hairstrand and slide comb down to base
» Remove comb at base and repeat from midstrand to ends
» Repeat as often as necessary until desired degree of backcombing is achieved
» Work toward crown, sides and nape

9. Define and detail to personalize design:

» Use tip of tail comb to separate hair
» Apply finishing products as needed

10. The finish displays a soft, airy, casual look.

COMPLETION	

» Discard single-use supplies
» Disinfect tools and multi-use supplies
» Disinfect workstation and arrange in proper order

25 mins
Suggested
Salon Speed

My Speed
_____
_____
_____

INSTRUCTIONS:

Record your time in comparison with the suggested salon speed. Then, list here how you could improve your performance.

_____

_____

_____

_____

ROUND BRUSH AND CURLING IRON

EXPLORE

Why do you think hairstylists use different types and sizes of brushes?

INSPIRE

Understanding which tools to use and how they can work together allows you to achieve the desired look.

ACHIEVE

Following this *Round Brush and Curling Iron Workshop*, you'll be able to:

>> Create a design with a progression of volume that moves away from the face using air forming and curling iron techniques

>> Air form a wave pattern at the sides using a 9-row brush

>> Air form a progression of volume using a round brush

>> Create a progression of volume with a curling iron

A combination of tools is used to create a design that moves away from the face.

A progression of volume, from overdirected at the front hairline to diminished at the nape, is achieved through air forming and curling iron techniques.

THERMAL-SETTING PROCEDURES –
AIR FORMING AND CURLING IRON

1-2. DISTRIBUTE/MOLD:
    Straight parallel | Curved parallel

3-5. SCALE/PART/APPLY:

    Partings
        Horizontal | Diagonal-forward | Vertical
    Rectangular bases
        1x half-off base | 1x on base | 1½x overdirected

9-ROW BRUSH	ROUND BRUSH	CURLING IRON

ROUND BRUSH AND CURLING IRON

Draw or fill in the boxes with the appropriate answers.

DESIGN DECISIONS

STRUCTURE	FORM/TEXTURE		
DISTRIBUTE			
AIR-FORMING PATTERN			
CURLING IRON PATTERN			
FINISH/DIRECTION			

Instructor Signature _____ Date _____

PERFORMANCE GUIDE

ROUND BRUSH AND CURLING IRON

View the video, complete the Design Decisions chart, then perform this workshop. Complete the self-check as you progress through the workshop.

45 mins
Suggested Salon Speed

PREPARATION	✔
	>> Assemble tools and products >> Set up workstation	☐

AIR FORMING — 9-ROW BRUSH

	1. **Section hair from center front hairline to occipital, and from center of occipital to hairline.**	☐
	2. **Air form nape and back using 9-row brush:** >> Lift base to create volume >> Position brush underneath hair to create curved end texture >> Dry base, midstrand and then ends >> Work from center to either side >> Work upward using same techniques from diagonal-forward and vertical partings	☐
	3. **Air form the lengths away from face at top:** >> Continue to create volume at the base and curved end texture	☐

4. **Air form first oblong on one side:**
   >> Create an oblong shape with bristles of brush
   >> Direct airflow into center of oblong to reinforce curved lines

5. **Air form second oblong in opposite direction:**
   >> Direct airflow in center of oblong to reinforce curved lines

6. **Air form alternating oblongs on opposite side.**

AIR FORMING — ROUND BRUSH

7. **A bricklay pattern is used to create a progression of volume from horizontal, diagonal-forward and vertical partings:**
   >> Round brush is used to establish direction and curl pattern
   >> Curling iron is used to reinforce and strengthen curl pattern
   >> Progression of base control is used from end texture in back, to exaggerated volume at front hairline

8. **Create curved end texture using half-off base control:**
   >> Position round brush underneath hair
   >> Rotate brush in a continuous motion from ends to base
   >> Work from center to either side
   >> Allow hair to cool before removing brush

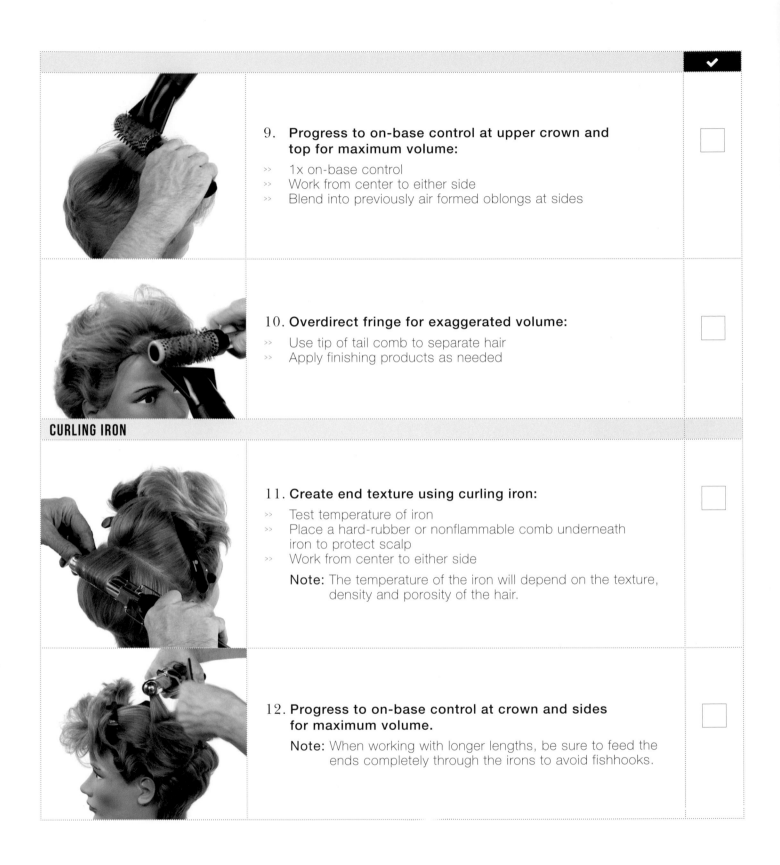

9. **Progress to on-base control at upper crown and top for maximum volume:**

   ›› 1x on-base control
   ›› Work from center to either side
   ›› Blend into previously air formed oblongs at sides

10. **Overdirect fringe for exaggerated volume:**

   ›› Use tip of tail comb to separate hair
   ›› Apply finishing products as needed

CURLING IRON

11. **Create end texture using curling iron:**

   ›› Test temperature of iron
   ›› Place a hard-rubber or nonflammable comb underneath iron to protect scalp
   ›› Work from center to either side

   Note: The temperature of the iron will depend on the texture, density and porosity of the hair.

12. **Progress to on-base control at crown and sides for maximum volume.**

   Note: When working with longer lengths, be sure to feed the ends completely through the irons to avoid fishhooks.

13. **Blend volume curls into alternating oblongs at sides:**
   >> Be careful not to disturb wave formation at sides

14. **Create an asymmetrical movement at front hairline using diagonal partings:**
   >> A portion of front hairline may be directed toward the face

FINISH — COMB-OUT

15. **Relax the set and break up surface texture using your fingers.**

16. **Backcomb surface of hair:**
   >> Use wide-tooth tail comb
   >> Work from center-front hairline to nape
   >> Keep base controls in mind when backcombing to achieve desired degree of volume

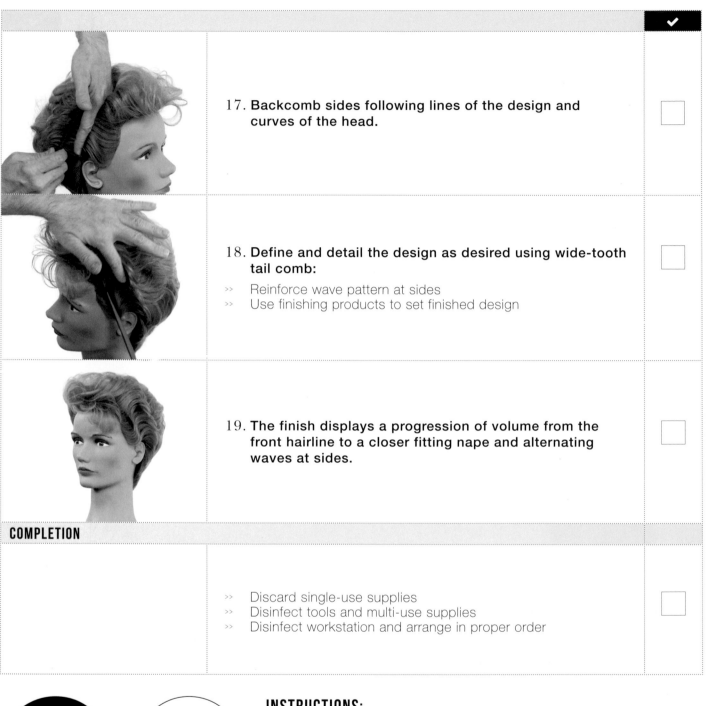

	✔
17. **Backcomb sides following lines of the design and curves of the head.**	☐
18. **Define and detail the design as desired using wide-tooth tail comb:** » Reinforce wave pattern at sides » Use finishing products to set finished design	☐
19. **The finish displays a progression of volume from the front hairline to a closer fitting nape and alternating waves at sides.**	☐

COMPLETION

» Discard single-use supplies » Disinfect tools and multi-use supplies » Disinfect workstation and arrange in proper order	☐

45 mins
Suggested Salon Speed

My Speed
_____
_____
_____

INSTRUCTIONS:
Record your time in comparison with the suggested salon speed. Then, list here how you could improve your performance.

_____
_____
_____
_____
_____

PRESS AND CURL

EXPLORE

How important do you think pressing and curling is as a service?

INSPIRE

Being proficient and confident in performing the press and curl service will not only boost your profits, but also help you gain a loyal client base.

ACHIEVE

Following this *Press and Curl Workshop,* you'll be able to:

>> Air form tightly curled hair with a 9-row brush

>> Demonstrate the double-press technique on tightly curled hair

>> Create a design with curved-under ends using a thermal iron

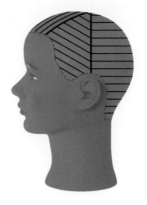
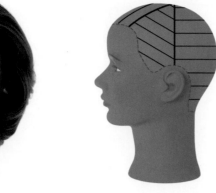
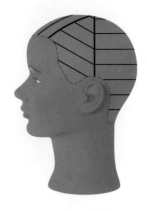

AIR FORMING   PRESSING   CURLING

The finish shows straightened lengths that move away from the face, with interior volume and a subtle bevel-under effect in the back.

This press and curl workshop is subdivided into three major areas: air forming, pressing and curling. The hair is sectioned in four sections from an off-center part. Horizontal partings are used in the back, while diagonal-back partings are used on the sides. For air forming, ½" (1.25 cm) partings are used, while ¼" (.6 cm) partings are used to press the hair. For the thermal iron technique, the size of the parting is in relation to the diameter of the thermal iron.

THERMAL-SETTING PROCEDURES – PRESS AND CURL

	AIR FORMING – 9-ROW	PRESSING COMB	THERMAL IRON
1-2. DISTRIBUTE/MOLD: Straight parallel	↓↓↓↓	↓↓↓↓	↓↓↓↓

3-5. SCALE/PART/APPLY:
Bevel-under effect │ Double-press technique
Ends technique

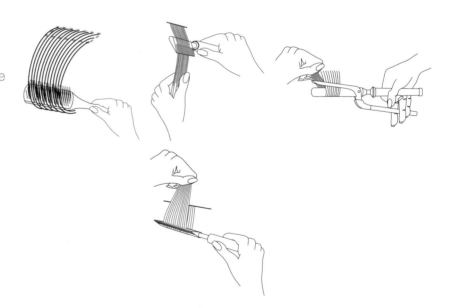

PRESS AND CURL

Draw or fill in the boxes with the appropriate answers.

DESIGN DECISIONS

STRUCTURE	FORM/TEXTURE		

AIR-FORMING PATTERN

PRESSING PATTERN

CURLING PATTERN

FINISH/DIRECTION

Instructor Signature _____ Date _____

PERFORMANCE GUIDE

PRESS AND CURL

View the video, complete the Design Decisions chart, then perform this workshop. Complete the self-check as you progress through the workshop.

1 hr
30 mins
Suggested
Salon Speed

PREPARATION	✔
>> Assemble tools and products >> Set up workstation	☐

DETANGLE – SECTION – AIR FORM

	1. **Detangle hair to prepare for air-forming procedure:** >> Work trom ends to base using a wide-tooth comb	☐
	2. **Section hair into 4 sections:** >> Off-center part from front hairline to crown >> Center part from crown to nape >> Apex to top of each ear	☐
	3. **Apply thermal protectant cream to hair:** >> Follow sanitation guidelines to remove cream from container >> Gently rub product in your hands >> Apply product from base to ends >> Distribute product through hair with wide-tooth comb from base to ends >> Complete each section	☐

4. Begin air forming hair in center nape with 9-row brush:

>> Release a ½" (1.25 cm) horizontal parting
>> Position 9-row brush underneath hair
>> Direct airflow on top of hair pointing nozzle downward and away from scalp
>> Dry the base, midstrand and ends
>> Rotate brush on ends in a circular motion to create a bevel-under effect

5. Work from center to either side using same air forming techniques.

6. Subdivide horizontal partings for control as you work upward:

>> Direct airflow on top of hair beginning at base and continuing through midstrand and ends
>> Rotate brush on ends to create a bevel-under effect

7. Complete the back using same air-forming techniques:

>> On last parting, combine both sections in order to avoid splits

8. **Air form left side beginning at bottom of section:**
   >> Diagonal-back partings
   >> Position 9-row brush under section of hair
   >> Direct airflow on top of section while drying base, midstrand and ends
   >> Rotate brush on ends to create a bevel-under effect

9. **Work upward using same air-forming procedures.**
   >> Subdivide partings for control
   >> Extend diagonal-back partings into back section to avoid splits

10. **Complete left side using same air-forming procedures.**

11. **Repeat same air-forming procedures from diagonal-back partings on opposite side.**

12. Subdivide hair into same 4 sections.

13. Release ¼" (.6 cm) horizontal parting at nape.

14. **Test temperature of pressing comb against white paper towel prior to applying to hair:**
    >> If paper towel remains white, pressing comb is safe to use and you may proceed
    >> If paper towel turns brown, allow pressing comb to cool and re-test

15. **Begin at center nape and press hair twice from underneath:**
    >> Insert teeth of comb underneath hairstrand near base
    >> Turn pressing comb and press hair using spine of comb while controlling ends
    >> Repeat

16. **Press same parting twice on top of strand:**
    >> Insert teeth of comb on top of hairstrand near base
    >> Turn pressing comb and press hair using spine of comb while controlling ends
    >> Repeat

    Note: This completes the double-press technique within the same section of hair.

17. **Work from center to one side, then other side using same double-press techniques:**
    - >> Be sure to test temperature of pressing comb

18. **Work upward using double-press technique from horizontal partings:**
    - >> Subdivide partings for control
    - >> Work from center to one side, then other side

19. **Complete the back using double-press technique.**

20. **Move to left side and press hair using double-press technique from diagonal-back partings:**
    - >> Begin at hairline in front of ear
    - >> Press twice underneath section of hair
    - >> Press twice on top of section of hair

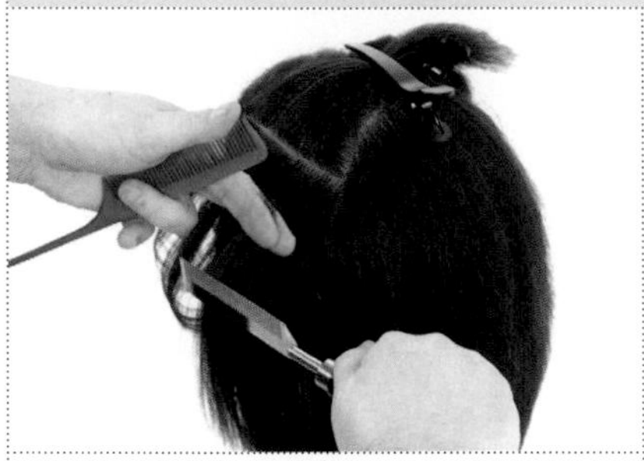

	✔

21. Subdivide partings for control as you work upward:

>> Use spine of comb to press hair
>> Remember to test temperature of pressing comb

☐

22. Complete left side using double-press technique.

☐

23. Repeat same double-press techniques on opposite side.

☐

24. Press perimeter hairline to blend bases:

>> Insert teeth of comb into hairline and turn comb to press hairline away from face
>> Work from front hairline to back

☐

CURL HAIR — BEVEL-UNDER

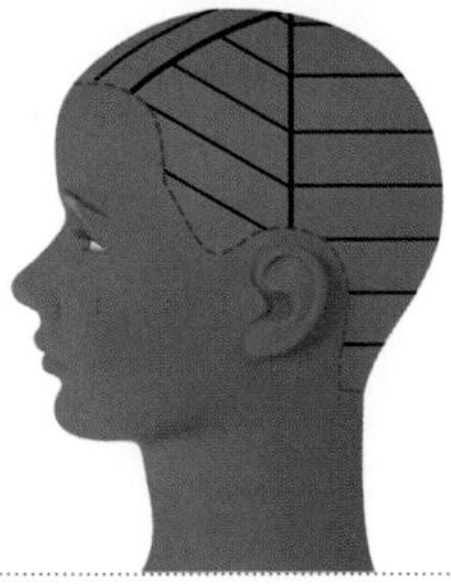

25. Subdivide hair using same sectioning pattern.

>> Horizontal and diagonal-back partings are used to curl the hair

☐

26. Test temperature of marcel iron:

>> If paper towel remains white, marcel iron is safe to use and you may proceed

>> If paper towel turns brown, allow marcel iron to cool and re-test

27. Begin to curl hair at nape from horizontal parting:

>> Use diameter of marcel iron as guide to determine width of base

>> Smooth surface of base using barrel of curling iron

>> Direct ends to one side, then click and turn iron to direct ends through iron

>> Work from center to each side using same marcel iron techniques

28. Continue to curl ends as you work up the back:

>> Horizontal partings

>> Subdivide for control

>> Test temperature of thermal iron

29. Complete back using same marcel iron techniques:

>> Combine both sections at crown to avoid splits

30. Curl left side using same marcel iron techniques from diagonal-back partings:

>> Protect face and scalp with a hard-rubber or nonflammable comb as needed

31. Work upward subdividing partings for control:

>> Test temperature of thermal iron
>> Protect scalp with a hard-rubber or nonflammable comb

32. Complete left side using same marcel iron techniques.

33. Repeat same marcel iron techniques on right side:

>> Diagonal partings
>> Protect scalp with a hard-rubber or nonflammable comb
>> Test temperature of thermal iron

FINISH – COMB-OUT

34. Relax curls using wide-tooth comb:

>> Work from front to center-back on each side

35. Define and detail the form:

>> Direct hair away from face, blending to sides and back
>> Use wide-tooth comb to create separated surface texture
>> Use finishing products as desired to support the finish

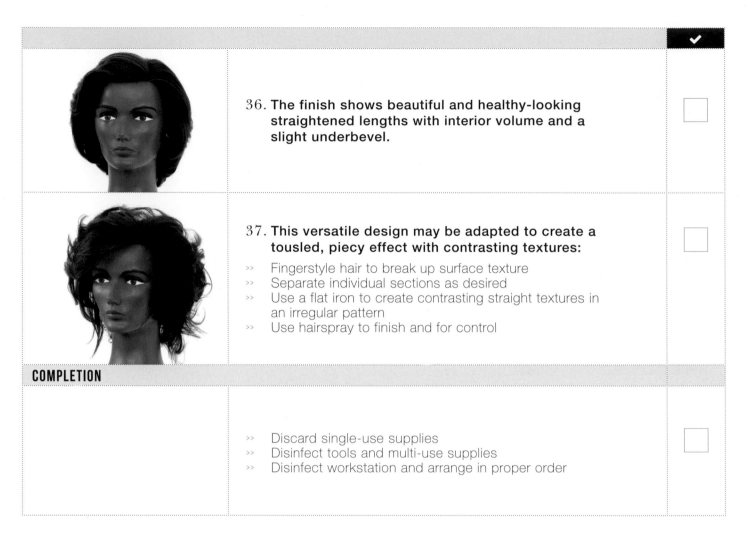

✓

36. **The finish shows beautiful and healthy-looking straightened lengths with interior volume and a slight underbevel.**

37. **This versatile design may be adapted to create a tousled, piecy effect with contrasting textures:**

>> Fingerstyle hair to break up surface texture
>> Separate individual sections as desired
>> Use a flat iron to create contrasting straight textures in an irregular pattern
>> Use hairspray to finish and for control

COMPLETION

>> Discard single-use supplies
>> Disinfect tools and multi-use supplies
>> Disinfect workstation and arrange in proper order

1 hr 30 mins
Suggested Salon Speed

My Speed
_____
_____
_____

INSTRUCTIONS:

Record your time in comparison with the suggested salon speed. Then, list here how you could improve your performance.

_____

_____

_____

_____

VARIATION – PRESS AND CURL – VOLUME AND INDENTATION

A variation on the press and curl technique to include indentation is available online.

MOLDING AND CURLING IRON

EXPLORE

Why is it necessary to have a strong foundation before a house is built?

INSPIRE

Creating the foundation of movement with a molded set will help guide you to create the finished curling iron set.

ACHIEVE

Following this *Molding and Curling Iron Workshop*, you'll be able to:

>> Create directional volume that moves away from the face by molding the hair and finishing with curling iron techniques

The finish shows interior volume that moves off the face, blending into a close-fitting contour.

Straight parallel distribution is used in the exterior. Directional distribution is used from an imaginary point of origin above the left eye to move hair away from the face. Rectangle-shaped bases are used for the curling iron set.

THERMAL SETTING PROCEDURES: MOLDING AND CURLING IRON

MOLDING   CURLING IRON

1-2. DISTRIBUTE/MOLD:
      Straight parallel │ Curved parallel

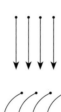

3.   SCALE: N/A

4.   PART:
      Horizontal │ Slight diagonal

5.   APPLY:
      Rectangle-shaped bases │ 1x half-off

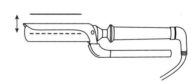

DESIGN DECISIONS CHART

MOLDING AND CURLING IRON

Draw or fill in the boxes with the appropriate answers.

DESIGN DECISIONS

STRUCTURE

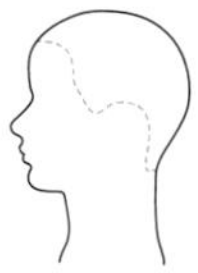

FORM/TEXTURE

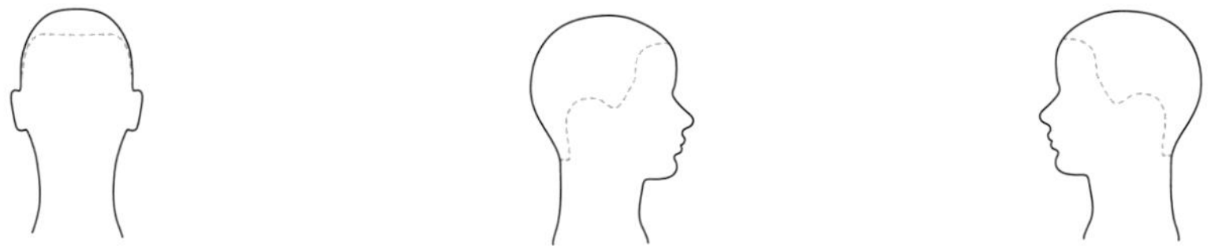

DISTRIBUTE/MOLD

CURLING PATTERN

FINISH/DIRECTION

Instructor Signature ______________________________ **Date** ______________

PERFORMANCE GUIDE
MOLDING AND CURLING IRON

View the video, complete the Design Decisions chart, then perform this workshop. Complete the self-check as you progress through the workshop.

45 mins
Suggested
Salon Speed

PREPARATION		✔
	>> Assemble tools and products >> Set up workstation	☐

DISTRIBUTE/MOLD

	1. **Apply styling liquid or cream to hair from base to ends:** >> Use comb to evenly distribute	☐
	2. **Straight and curved parallel distribution is used to mold hair.**	
	3. **Distribute and mold nape:** >> Use fine teeth of comb >> Flatten hair vertically downward >> Use index finger to maintain tension	☐
	4. **Mold right side:** >> Horizontal partings >> Mold vertically downward >> Work from front hairline to center back >> Work around ear blending into nape	☐

5. Mold left side from front hairline to center back.

6. Mold upward to crest area:
   >> Work from front hairline to center back, blending to previously molded hair

7. An imaginary point of origin above left eye is used to establish movement in interior.

8. Mold hair at front hairline directionally back away from face:
   >> Use finger to control molding

9. Mold curved parallel lines to blend into sides and exterior.

DRY HAIR   ✔

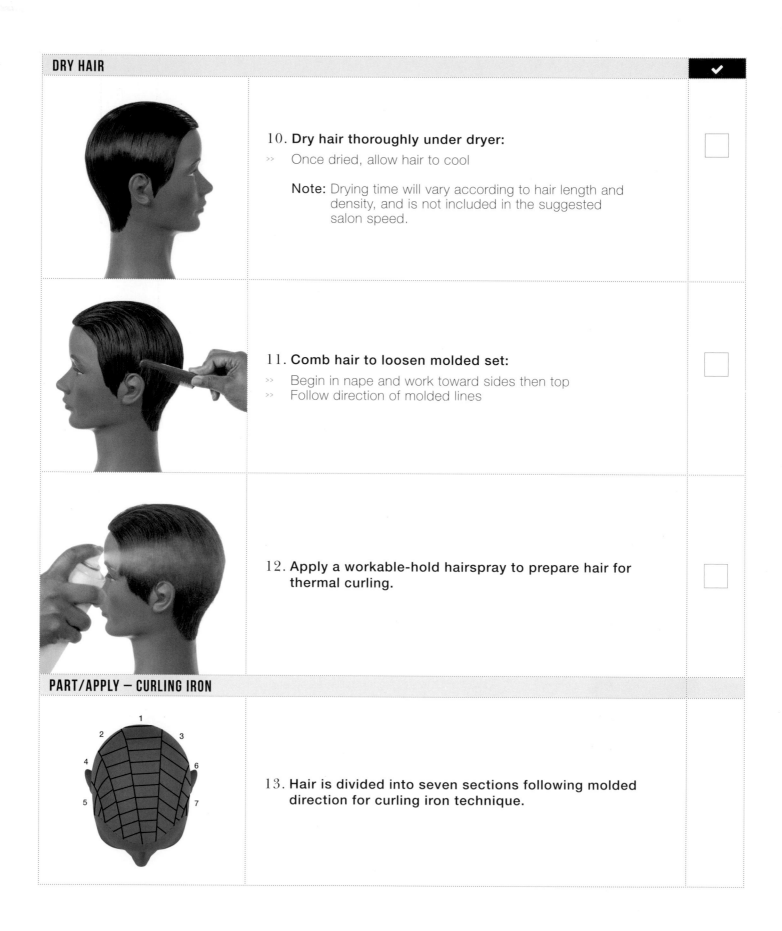

10. **Dry hair thoroughly under dryer:**
    >> Once dried, allow hair to cool

    Note: Drying time will vary according to hair length and
    density, and is not included in the suggested
    salon speed.

11. **Comb hair to loosen molded set:**
    >> Begin in nape and work toward sides then top
    >> Follow direction of molded lines

12. **Apply a workable-hold hairspray to prepare hair for
    thermal curling.**

PART/APPLY – CURLING IRON

13. **Hair is divided into seven sections following molded
    direction for curling iron technique.**

14. Begin curling iron technique at front hairline (Section 1):

>> Curl the ends
>> Support base and protect scalp with hard-rubber or nonflammable comb

15. Work toward crown using same curling iron procedures.

16. Blend shorter exterior lengths with smaller-diameter curling iron.

17. Curl Section 2:

>> Adjust angle of partings as you work from front hairline to back

18. Switch to smaller-diameter iron to blend to shorter lengths.

19. Repeat curling iron techniques on Section 3 on opposite side.

20. Curl Section 4 working from front hairline to back.

21. **Curl Section 5:**
    >> If lengths are too short, use tip of tail comb to part and direct shorter lengths

22. Repeat same curling iron techniques on opposite side with Sections 6 and 7.

FINISH – COMB-OUT ✔

23. Relax and detail hair:
>> Begin at nape working toward front hairline
>> Break up the texture to define and detail the design

☐

24. The finish shows a soft, textured look with a progression of curls from the front hairline to the back.

☐

COMPLETION

>> Discard single-use supplies
>> Disinfect tools and multi-use supplies
>> Disinfect workstation and arrange in proper order

☐

45 mins
Suggested Salon Speed

My Speed
_____
_____
_____

INSTRUCTIONS:
Record your time in comparison with the suggested salon speed. Then, list here how you could improve your performance.

_____
_____
_____
_____
_____

➤➤ 107^c GLOSSARY/INDEX

Scale 35, 37
Carving shapes in the proper size and proportion to establish the lines of the design; also known as section.

Scrunching 173
Form of fingerstyling; involves gently squeezing the hair lengths as the hair is dried using a diffuser to introduce a texture pattern that the hair responds to naturally.

Semi Stand-Up Pincurl 90
Transitional pincurls; not quite a stand-up curl and not quite a flat curl; creates a blend or transition from areas of volume to areas of closeness.

Setting Procedures 35
In hair design, procedures used that lead to predictable results; distribute, mold, scale, part and apply.

Shape 8, 9
A two-dimensional outline of form as seen in its silhouette or outer boundary; the contour of an object.

Skip Waves 148
Wave pattern composed of two alternating oblongs connected by a ridge; one oblong is molded, and one is set.

Soft Press 183
Pressing the hair once on each side with less pressure and heat using a pressing comb.

Stem 43
Hair between the scalp and the first turn of the hair around the roller, thermal iron and round brush; the stem determines the amount of movement of the section of hair; also known as the arc.

Straight Indentation 82
Base control, which creates hollowness and depression; base and stem are flat, and the ends turn upward.

Straight Volume 82
Base control, which creates lift and fullness; base and strand are lifted, and the ends turn under.

Straight Volume Pincurl 90
Large stand-up pincurls, achieving a similar effect to hair wound around roller but results in weaker (less) volume; also called stand-up, cascade and barrel pincurls.

Texture 8, 10
Visual appearance or feel of a surface; hair's surface appearance can be unactivated (smooth) or activated (rough).

Texture Character 10
Refers to the shape of the texture pattern; created by the shape and position of the tool along the hairstrand.

Texture Speed 11
Describes the dimension of the texture pattern; can range from slow waves to fast, highly activated curls.

Thermal Curling 177
The process of temporarily adding curl texture to dry hair using heated irons (electric or stove heated).

Thermal Designing 7, 170
Technique of drying and/or designing hair by using a hand-held dryer while simultaneously using the fingers, a variety of brushes, pressing comb and/or a thermal iron; also called thermal styling.

Thermal Protectant 30
Product used to prepare and protect hair against heat styling.

Trapezoid 38
A geometric shape with two unequal, parallel sides and two equal, nonparallel sides.

Triangle 38
A geometric three-sided shape.

Underdirected 84, 103
Tool or curl sits in the lower portion of the base but not on or below the parting; results in reduced volume and base strength.

Undulating Irons 28
Design tool that consists of two curved irons used to create an "S" pattern in the hair.

Vent Brush 25
Brush that allows the greatest airflow to the hair so that the lengths can be dried quickly while directing into the lines of the design.

Volume 8
Mass or fullness in a design.

Volume Oblong 110, 111
Setting begins at the convex end with partings made at a 45° angle in the first direction, with a tool rolled under to lift the base.

Volume Pincurl 90, 91, 113, 115
Base and stem (arc) are lifted away from the head, and the circle turns under; used to create fullness and height.

Wave Pattern 110
Two or more oblongs set in alternating (opposite) directions.

Wet Design 7
Refers to the area of hair designing in which the hair is manipulated into the desired shapes and movements while wet and then allowed to dry; also known as wet styling.

Wide-Tooth Tail Comb 24
Used for backcombing and finishing techniques; wide-spaced teeth create texture patterns that reflect the shape and interval of the teeth; also known as a rake comb.

PIVOT POINT

 ACKNOWLEDGMENTS

Pivot Point Fundamentals is designed to provide education to undergraduate students to help prepare them for licensure and an entry-level position in the cosmetology field. An undertaking of this magnitude requires the expertise and cooperation of many people who are experts in their field. Pivot Point takes pride in our internal team of educators who develop cosmetology, esthetics and nails education, along with our print and digital experts, designers, editors, illustrators and video producers. Pivot Point would like to express our many thanks to these talented individuals who have devoted themselves to the business of beauty, lifelong learning and especially for help raising the bar for future professionals in our industry.

EDUCATION DEVELOPMENT	**Janet Fisher // Sabine Held-Perez // Vasiliki A. Stavrakis**
	Markel Artwell
	Eileen Dubelbeis
	Brian Fallon
	Melissa Holmes
	Lisa Luppino
	Paul Suttles
	Amy Gallagher
	Lisa Kersting
	Jamie Nabielec
	Vic Piccolotto
	Ericka Thelin
	Jane Wegner

EDITORIAL	**Maureen Spurr // Wm. Bullion // Deidre Glover**
	Liz Bagby
	Jack Bernin
	Lori Chapman

DESIGN & PRODUCTION	**Jennifer Eckstein // Rick Russell // Danya Shaikh**
	Joanna Jakubowicz
	Denise Podlin
	Annette Baase
	Agnieszka Hansen
	Kristine Palmer
	Tiffany Wu

PROJECT MANAGEMENT	**Jenny Allen // Ken Wegrzyn**

DIGITAL DEVELOPMENT	John Bernin
	Javed Fouch
	Anna Fehr
	Matt McCarthy
	Marcia Noriega
	Corey Passage
	Herb Potzus

Pivot Point also wishes to take this opportunity to acknowledge the many contributors and product concept testers who helped make this program possible.

INDUSTRY CONTRIBUTORS

Linda Burmeister
Esthetics

Jeanne Braa Foster
Dr. Dean Foster
Eyes on Cancer

Mandy Gross
Nails

Andrea D. Kelly, MA, MSW
University of Delaware

Rosanne Kinley
Infection Control
National Interstate Council

Lynn Maestro
Cirépil by Perron Rigot, Paris

Andrzej Matracki
World and European
Men's Champion

MODERN SALON

Rachel Molepske
Look Good Feel Better, PBA
CUT IT OUT, PBA

Peggy Moon
Liaison to Regulatory and Testing

Robert Richards
Fashion Illustrations

Clif St. Germain, Ph.D
Educational Consultant

Andis Company

International Dermal Institute

HairUWear Inc.

Lock & Loaded Men's Grooming

PRODUCT CONCEPT TESTING

Central Carolina
Community College
Millington, North Carolina

Gateway Community Colleges
Phoenix, Arizona

MC College
Edmonton, Alberta

Metro Beauty Academy
Allentown, Pennsylvania

Rowan Cabarrus Community
College
Kannapolis, North Carolina

Sunstate Academy of
Cosmetology and Massage
Ft. Myers, Florida

Summit Salon Academy
Kokomo, Indiana

TONI&GUY Hairdressing Academy
Costa Mesa, California
Plano, Texas

Xenon Academy
Omaha, NE
Grand Island, NE

LEADERSHIP TEAM

Robert Passage
Chairman and CEO

Robert J. Sieh
Senior Vice President,
Finance and Operations

Judy Rambert
Vice President, Education

Kevin Cameron
Senior Vice President,
Education and Marketing

R.W. Miller
Vice President, Domestic Sales
and Field Education

Jan Laan
Vice President, International
Business Development

Katy O'Mahony
Director, Human Resources

In addition, we give special thanks to the North American Regulating agencies whose careful work protects us as well as our clients, enhancing the high quality of our work. These agencies include Occupational Health and Safety Agency (OSHA) and the U.S. Environmental Protection Agency (EPA). *Pivot Point Fundamentals*™ promotes use of their policies and procedures.

Pivot Point International would like to express our SPECIAL THANKS to the inspired visual artisans of Creative Commons, without whose talents this book of beauty would not be possible.